W9-CRX-111

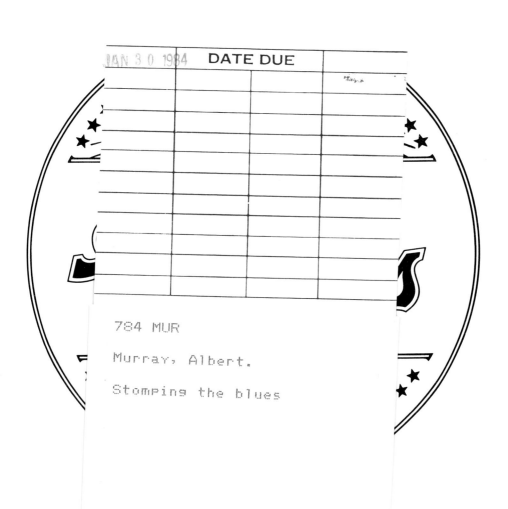

Also by Albert Murray

The Omni-Americans
South to a Very Old Place
The Hero and the Blues
Train Whistle Guitar

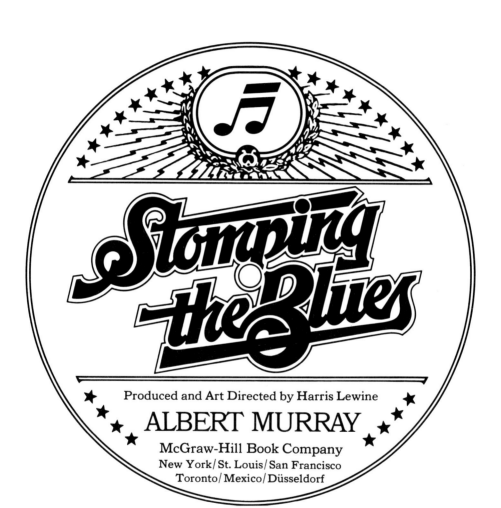

Stomping the Blues

Produced and Art Directed by Harris Lewine

ALBERT MURRAY

McGraw-Hill Book Company

New York/St. Louis/San Francisco
Toronto/Mexico/Düsseldorf

123456789 R A B P 79876
Design by Alan Peckolick

Library of Congress Cataloging in Publication Data

Murray, Albert.
Stomping the blues.

Discography: p.
Includes index.
1.   Blues (Songs, etc.)—United States—History
and criticism.   I.   Title.
ML3561.B63M9   784   76-14949
ISBN 0-07-044074-3

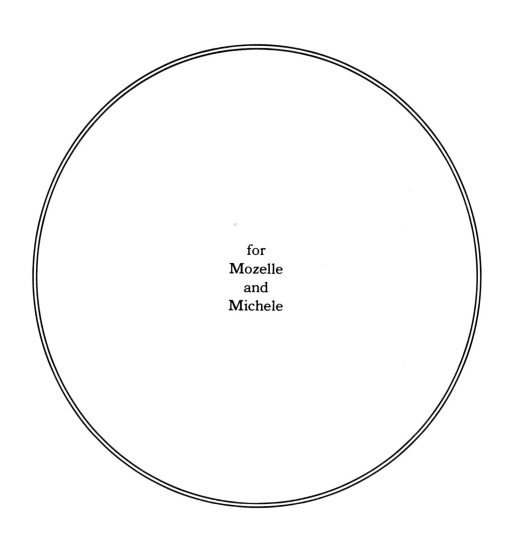

for
Mozelle
and
Michele

Contents

The Blues
as Such

Sometimes you forget all about them in spite of yourself, but all too often the very first thing you realize when you wake up is that they are there again, settling in like bad weather, hovering like plague-bearing insects, swarming precisely as if they were indeed blue demons dispatched on their mission of harassment by none other than the Chief Red Devil of all devils himself; and yet perhaps as often as not it is also as if they squat obscene and vulturelike, waiting and watching you and preening themselves at the same time, their long rubbery necks writhing as if floating.

Not that they are ever actually seen. They are always said to be blue, even as common-variety ghosts are always said to be at least somewhat gray. But being absolutely insubstantial, they are in fact completely invisible for all that everybody seems to have the distinct impression that they are always very small and not only plural but so numerous as to be numberless.

Still even as they are represented as teeming, swarming, and writhing nobody ever describes how they actually look. Because they have no image. Thus they do not appear and disappear. They are there because they have already come, and they linger somewhat as if clinging with tentacles, and they go, mostly when driven. But never soon enough. Nor do they ever seem to go far enough away even so. Once they have been there they only shift from the foreground to the background, and maybe you forget about them for the time being, but only for the time being.

All anybody ever presumes to describe with any precision is how you are likely to feel when they are present. You become afflicted as if infected by some miasma-generating microbe. You feel down-hearted and uncertain. You are woebegone and anxiety-ridden. So much so that you would think that their characteristic coloration would be something suggesting the grayness of low-hanging clouds rather than blue. But in truth nobody ever seems to give that matter any thought at all, and there is even less concern about which specific shade of blue is involved. At the same time, however, nobody ever confuses anything about their behavior with the silky blueness of high and cloudless skies either.

They are also absolutely noiseless at all times. Their movements make no sound whatsoever. And they are evidently voiceless. They are said to speak, but only in the silent language of spirits. So even when they are quoted as if verbatim, you know the speaker is paraphrasing, because the accent and tone and even the volume and timbre are always very obvious stylizations of a voice all too obviously his own. Moreover, no matter how concrete the refer-ences, you already know very well that the statement is meant only to be taken as allegorical. (Item: When Jimmy Rushing sings, "Good morning, blues. Blues how do you do? Blues say, 'I feel all right but I come to worry you,'" the reply is given as if literal but not only is the voice still Rushing's, there is also no confusion at all when the singular I is used instead of the plural we.)

Nor do they ever seem to shock and terrify as some specters sometimes do (as often by simply vanishing and reappearing and vanishing into thin air again as by popping into uncertain view from nowhere in the first place). You know they are there only because you feel their presence in the atmosphere once more as you did the time before and the time before that; because every-thing, which is to say time itself, has somehow become heavy with vague but dire and disconcerting forebodings of impending frustra-tion leading perhaps to ultimate doom. So sometimes at first it is as if you yourself have been draped with a leaden invisible net. Then you realize that you don't feel so good anymore, not because all at once you have been stricken but because a dull and unspecific ache is beginning to throb. Then sometimes you feel yourself be-coming rueful, or glum, or sometimes either sullen, mean, and downright evil on the one hand or weak in the stomach and knees on the other.

4

Sometimes it is as if they themselves actually generate and inflict misery upon their victims much the same as pathogenic bacteria cause infection. But not always. Perhaps most often it is as if their primary purpose is to becloud your outlook by foreshadowing misfortune, and there are also times when they seem to come along with whatever the trouble is, or to issue from it not unlike the side effects that are really only the symptoms of far more serious physical ailments.

Also, as is likewise the case with many physical afflictions, sometimes you already know the cause as well as you know the symptoms. Because all too often they are back again for exactly the same reason that they came to be there the times before. Not always, to be sure. But often enough for the consideration to be automatic. Indeed it may well be that the element of déjà vu is sometimes the source of as much anguish and hopelessness as the actual causal incident, if not more. Because it almost inevitably suggests (especially to those who have not yet come to realize that even in the best of times the blues are only at bay and are thus always somewhere in the not-too-distant background) that the mishap of the moment is but the latest episode in a string of misfortunes that are so persistent as to amount to a curse, and maybe even an ancestral curse at that.

But no matter how they come to be there again, the main thing about them is all the botheration they bring, and your most immediate concern is how to dislodge them before the botheration degenerates into utter hopelessness. So the very first problem that it all adds up to is as specific as is the ghostlike vagueness of their very existence, (which not everybody accepts as such anyway). What it requires is the primordial and ever persistent effort to purify the environment once more.

As in Oedipus Rex, for instance, which begins with a chorus of suppliants lamenting a curse that hangs over the city-state of Thebes and beseeching the hero/king to seek out and dispatch the menace and restore good times. As in the Wasteland episode in the medieval romance of the Quest in which the knight-errant comes into a region whose inhabitants are suffering under a blight because their ruler, known as the Fisher-King, is apparently bewitched and his impotence extends not only to the housewives but also to the cattle, the fields, and even the streams. As in Shake-

5

speare's Hamlet, *in which the young prince is charged by the ghost of his late father to rid the kingdom of Denmark of the evil forces that dominate it.*

Also always absolutely inseparable from all such predicaments and requirements is the most fundamental of all existential imperatives: affirmation, which is to say, reaffirmation and continuity in the face of adversity. Indeed, what with the blues (whether known by that or any other name) always somewhere either in the foreground or the background, reaffirmation is precisely the contingency upon which the very survival of man as human being, however normally unsatisfied and abnormally wretched, is predicated.

No wonder Hamlet came to debate with himself whether to be or not to be. Nor was it, or is it, a question of judging whether life is or is not worth living. Not in the academic sense of Albert Camus's concern with the intrinsic absurdity of existence per se. Hamlet's was whether things are worth all the trouble and struggle. Which is also what the question is when you wake up with the blues there again, not only all around your bed but also inside your head as well, as if trying to make you wish that you were dead or had never been born.

The Blues
Face to Face

S ometimes exposure through forthright acknowledgment of their unwelcome presence is enough to purge the immediate atmosphere, and no further confrontation is necessary. At such times they seem to vanish very much the way ghosts are said to do at the slightest indication that for all their notorious invisibility they have been discovered. There are times as a matter of fact when all it seems to take is the pronunciation (or mispronunciation) of their name with the proper overtones. Quite often not only will a few well-chosen epithets and outrageous hyperboles do the trick, but even a firmly pointed, sternly aimed finger.

Sometimes, since it is assumed that to know a name is also to be onto the game, the merest threat of revealing their diabolical identities and intentions through full-scale description is even more effective. Nor is bold and blatant misdefinition any less. Moreover when descriptions and definitions involve numbers of any kind, nothing less than instant terror is the most likely response, even when the numbers are patently phony (perhaps because the inevitable effect of enumeration and measurement is to reduce the infinity of the invisible to the finite and hence to modality, which after all is not only discernible but also controllable, and thus to mortality!).

Another form of acknowledgment and exposure is imitation, which includes mockery as well as mimickry. Because imitation, it should not be forgotten, whether with sound or by movement, is representation, which is to say reenactment, which of its very nature is obviously also the most graphic description and thus also the most specific definition. Which is bad enough. But perhaps far worse is casual mimickry, which even when it is relatively exact is an act of defiance to say the least. As for deliberately distor mimickry, not only is it outright misrepresentation (and t naked misidentification and misdefinition), but it is also undi guised defiance become downright mockery expressing contempt and even disdain.

Where there is bare-faced mockery the depth of the resistance goes without saying. And the same holds true in the case of malediction, or bad-mouthing, which in addition to loudmouthing or damnation by diatribe and vilification also includes insinuation and scandalous innuendo. The main thing, whatever the form, is resistance if not hostility. Because the whole point is not to give in and let them get you down. Nor is a flamboyant display of militant determination necessarily more effective than is cool resolution. Sometimes a carefully controlled frown or even the faintest of supercilious smiles will work as much havoc as a scream or a shout.

Nor does an entirely phony show or gesture of belligerent opposition seem to carry any less impact than the real thing. It is in fact as if the difference were not even discernible. But when you come down to fundamentals, it is precisely the spirit and not the concrete substance which counts in such confrontations, for the spirit, after all, is not only what is threatened but is also the very part of you that is assumed to be most vulnerable. For what is ultimately at stake is morale, which is to say the will to persevere, the disposition to persist and perhaps prevail; and what must be avoided by all means is a failure of nerve.

There are also other counteragents. There is voodooism, for instance. Many people seem to take it completely for granted that most if not all of their troubles have been brought on by sorcery of one kind or another. Such people regard the spell of the blues as a magical curse or fix instigated by enemy conjuration. Thus even if such people describe themselves as being haunted by blue demons they think of them as coming not from the Devil or even from some natural misfortune but from some specific potion, gris-gris, jomo, charm, or talisman, which can be counteracted only with the aid of a voodoo queen or madam (or somewhat less often, a voodoo king, doctor, witchdoctor, or snakedoctor) whose powers of conjuration are superior.

10

A world-renowned stomping place on Lenox Avenue at 140th Street, from 1926–59, where the music of the great dance orchestras was always at its best. Also known as The Home of Happy Feet and as The Track. The ballroom floor was a block long with a double bandstand to accommodate the two orchestras that usually played alternating sets.

(Top) Inside the Savoy. (Bottom, and opposite page) Saturday Night *pas de deux* uptown any night. Confrontation . . . improvisation . . . affirmation . . . celebration.

Most people, however, seem to feel that you might as well try to deal directly with the blues in the first place as become ensnarled in the endless network of superstition and intimidation upon which voodooism is predicated. To them the voodoo madam and the snakedoctor are if anything even more troublesome than the blues as such. Furthermore, what is to stop the voodoo madam/doctor from replacing the existing fix with one of his or her own? Not that most people are as free of voodoo-derived, or in any case voodoolike, fetishism as they perhaps like to think, as you have only to look at all the good-luck charms and signs around you everywhere every day to realize.

Whiskey, gin, brandy, vodka, wines, and other alcoholic beverages and concoctions are also traditional antidotes, or in any case personal fortifications, against the pernicious effects of the blues. And so are narcotics. But while for many people the stimulation of liquor and/or drugs is often sufficient to get them going or sometimes even to help them through many very difficult situations, the problem for countless others is not only that such stimulation is not enough but when it subsides you are likely to find the same old blues still very much there and indeed nagging at you worse than ever, not to mention how they thrive and multiply on the nourishment of your hangover. Moreover, perhaps the most obvious of all chronic blues casualties are those who are driven to alcoholism or drug addiction—which is to say, into the vicious circle of intoxification and depression.

●

But of all the age-old ways of dispelling the ominous atmosphere that comes along with the blues, the one most people seem to have found to be most consistently effective all told also turns out to be essentially compatible with a great majority of the positive impulses, urges, drives, cravings, needs, desires, and hence the definitive purposes, goals, and ideals of their existence. Nor should its identification come as a surprise to sufficiently attentive students of culture and civilization, and certainly not to students of the nature and function of aesthetics. The blues counteragent that is so much a part of many people's equipment for living that they hardly ever think about it as such anymore is that artful and sometimes seemingly magical combination of idiomatic incantation and percussion that creates the dance-oriented good-

16

time music also known as the blues.

Hence the dance hall as temple. Hence all the ceremonially deliberate drag steps and shaking and grinding movements during, say, the old downhome Saturday Night Function, and all the sacramental strutting and swinging along with all the elegant stomping every night at such long-since-consecrated ballrooms as, say, the old Savoy, once the glory of uptown Manhattan. And hence in consequence the fundamental function of the blues musician (also known as the jazz musician), the most obvious as well as the most pragmatic mission of whose performance is not only to drive the blues away and hold them at bay at least for the time being, but also to evoke an ambiance of Dionysian revelry in the process.

Which is to say, even as such blues (or jazz) performers as the appropriately legendary Buddy Bolden, the improbable but undeniable Jelly Roll Morton, the primordially regal Bessie Smith, played their usual engagements as dance-hall, night-club, and vaudeville entertainers, they were at the same time fulfilling a central role in a ceremony that was at once a purification rite and a celebration the festive earthiness of which was tantamount to a fertility ritual.

Ballroom dances, which like house-party dances probably represent the most comprehensive elaboration and refinement of communal dancing, are of their very nature festive occasions. They are always held in celebration of something. Sometimes they celebrate victory in combat, sports, and other contests. They also celebrate achievements in business, politics, and the arts, among other things. Then there are all the traditional events, such as birthdays, marriages, graduations, and all the seasonal and official red-letter anniversaries. The difference between blues-oriented ballroom dances and the others, however, is of fundamental significance. Customarily, in keeping with the one-dimensional frivolity of the proceedings, the music for the others is light, airy, gay, conventional, in a word, anything but serious. Whereas not only do a number of blues lyrics express an urgent and unmistakable concern with defeat, disappointment, betrayal, misfortune, not excluding death; but even the most exuberant stomp rendition is likely to contain some trace of sadness as a sobering reminder that life is at bottom, for all the very best of good times, a never-ending struggle.

17

Bessie Smith, 1894-1937, also billed as the Empress of the Blues; and Louis Armstrong, 1900-71, who could conjure up good times with the magical art of music.

And yet the irrepressible joyousness, the downright exhilaration, the rapturous delight in sheer physical existence, like the elegant jocularity and hearty nonsense that are no less characteristic of blues music, are unsurpassed by any other dance music in the world. Still, the captivating elegance that always seems so entirely innate to blues-idiom dance movement is something earned in a context of antagonism. Not unlike the parade-ground-oriented sporty limp walk of the epic hero and the championship athlete, it has been achieved through the manifestation of grace under pressure such as qualifies the matador, for example, for his suit of lights and his pigtail.

But as to the matter of dispersing gloom and spreading glee, evidence in favor of the sorcery of Madam Marie Laveau, also known as the Widow Paris, the most notorious New Orleans voodoo queen, and the mojo hands of Doctor Jim Alexander, né Charles La Fountain, also known as Indian Jim, her male counterpart, is questionable to say the very least. Testimony that the dance-beat incantation and percussion of Bessie Smith and Louis Armstrong almost always worked as advertised is universal.

The Blue Devils
and the
Holy Ghost

There are blue devils, and there is also the Holy Ghost. Thus not everybody defines blues music and blues-idiom dance movements in the same terms. What the dance hall seems always to have suggested to the ministers and elders of most downhome churches, for instance, is the exact opposite of a locale for a purification ritual. To them any secular dancing place is a House of Sin and Folly, a Den of Iniquity, a Writhing Hellhole, where the weaknesses of the flesh are indulged to the ruination of the mind and body and eternal damnation of the soul. Which is also to say that all such places are also gateways to the downward path to everlasting torment in the fire and brimstone that is the certain fate of all sinners.

The vitriolic prayers and sermons against ballroom dances in general and the denunciation of the old downhome Saturday Night Function in particular express a preoccupation that amounts to obsession. By contrast, the all but total absence of any urgent concern about all of the incontestably pagan fetishism that is almost as explicit as implicit in the widespread involvement with good-luck charms, love potions, effigies, and all the other magical trinkets and devices that are so prevalent even among some regular churchgoers is nothing short of remarkable. Furthermore, for all the didactic allusions to the unrelenting opposition of the Prophets to idolatry and soothsaying in Biblical times, traditional downhome sermons by and large tend to ignore contemporary fortunetellers and voodoo madams and snakedoctors. Not so in the case of the local honky-tonk and dance-hall proprietors. They are castigated weekly, often by name.

As for the Saturday Night Function being a ritual to purge the atmosphere of baleful spirits, church-oriented downhome people are likely to express a very firm conviction that such diabolical afflictions exist only in the bad conscience of the sinful in the first place. In their view such pestilential vexations are not sent from the Devil (whose earthly stock in trade is enticement), but are manifestations of the wrath of the Lord, and they are only harbingers of the miseries sinners bring upon themselves by remaining outside the almighty protection of God's Word as represented by the church.

The problem as defined from the pulpit is not the purgation of the environment, which is inherently evil, but rather the purification of yourself and fortification against temptation. Because the only salvation of your soul is through conversion, baptism, and devotion. Not that you will never feel dejected again. But not because of the blues. When church members feel downcast it is because they have somehow displeased God, in whose sight mortal flesh must always feel itself unworthy even at best. In any case, the all but impossible way to Grace is through the denial of sensual gratification, never through the Garden of Earthly Delights.

It is accordingly precisely the blues musician's capacity to generate merriment that downhome church elders have always condemned first of all. They have never taken such incantation and percussion as being anything even remotely defiant or in any way antagonistic to any demons whatsoever. On the contrary, to them it is the Devil's very own music. They have always been completely certain that it not only brings out the devilment inherent in the weakness of the flesh (born as it is in sin and shaped in iniquity), but is also a call to the Devil himself to come forth and reign on earth as in Pandemonium.

Which is not to say that the church service is without its own merriment. Along with all the solemn rituals of devotion through submissive obedience there is also a fundamental requirement for the faithful to make a joyful noise unto the everlasting Glory of God. Thus there is also good-time music that has no less of a place in the regular order of devotional services than the prayers, solemn hymns and anthems, spirituals, sermons, and the Amen Corner chants and moans. Nor is it at all unusual for the hand

Old downhome church.

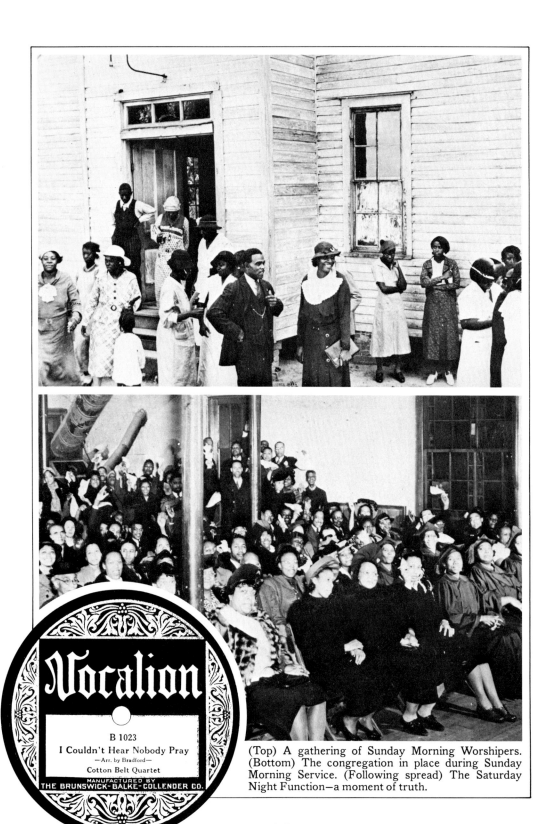

Vocalion

B 1023
I Couldn't Hear Nobody Pray
—Arr. by Bradford—
Cotton Belt Quartet

MANUFACTURED BY
THE BRUNSWICK-BALKE-COLLENDER CO.

(Top) A gathering of Sunday Morning Worshipers.
(Bottom) The congregation in place during Sunday
Morning Service. (Following spread) The Saturday
Night Function—a moment of truth.

clapping and foot shuffling plus rocking and rolling of a congregation singing chorus after medium to uptempo chorus of, say, *I
Couldn't Hear Nobody Pray* or *Just a Closer Walk with Thee,* to
generate paroxysms of ecstasy that exceed anything that happens
in the most gutbucket-oriented of honky-tonks. On occasion the
Bacchanalian music of the Saturday Night Function becomes
forthrightly orgiastic, as everybody not only knows but expects.
But even so, nobody is likely to compare the highly stylized intensity of the most lascivious honky-tonk dance movements with what
happens when a Sunday Morning worshiper is allowed to shout
until he or she begins speaking in unknown tongues because possessed by the Holy Ghost.

In point of fact, traditionally the highest praise given a blues
musician has been the declaration that he can make a dance hall
rock and roll like a downhome church during revival time. But
then many of the elements of blues music seem to have been
derived from the downhome church in the first place. After all,
such is the nature of the blues musician's development that even
when he or she did not begin as a church musician, he or she is
likely to have been conditioned by church music from infancy to a
far greater extent than by blues music as such. There are, it should
be remembered, no age limits on church attendance or church
music. Whereas during the childhood of all the musicians whose
work now represents the classics of the idiom, blues music was
considered to be so specifically adult that as a rule children were
not even permitted to listen to it freely, and for the most part were
absolutely forbidden to go anywhere near the festivities of the
Saturday Night Function until they were of age.

In any case, not a few of the idiomatic elements now considered
to be components of the definitive devices of blues musicianship
were already conventions of long standing among downhome
church musicians long before Buddy Bolden, Jelly Roll Morton,
King Oliver, W. C. Handy, and Ma Rainey came to apply them to
the dance hall. Whatever were the ultimate origins of the solo-
call/ensemble-riff-response pattern, for example, the chances are
that blues musicians adapted it from such church renditions as the
following:

Solo-call: *On the mountain.*
Congregation: *I couldn't hear nobody pray.*

27

Solo: *In the valley.*
Riff: *Couldn't hear nobody.*
Solo: *On my kneehees.*
Riff: *Couldn't hear nobody.*
Solo: *With my Jesus.*
Riff: *Couldn't hear nobody.*
Solo: *Oh, Lord.*
Riff: *I couldn't hear nobody.*
Solo: *Oh, Lordahawd!!!*
Riff: *Couldn't hear nobody pray.*
Everybody: *Way down yonder by myself
I couldn't hear nobody pray.*

Incidentally, the primary effect of barrelhousing and ragging and jazzing is not to make honky-tonk music more intrinsically dance-oriented than church music, but to make it more secular, which is to say, more appropriate to secular circumstances, attitudes and choreography. Downhome church music (by which is meant the conventional music of southern U.S. Negro Protestants) is not of its nature fundamentally less dance-beat-oriented, it simply inspires a different mode of dance, a sacred or holy as opposed to a secular or profane movement, a difference which is sometimes a matter of very delicate nuance. Indeed, sometimes only the initiated can make the distinctions. But churchfolks are always very much aware of them, and so are blues musicians for the most part, or at least so they used to be in the old days before certain gospel-fad pop hits popularized by Ray Charles and James Brown, and Aretha Franklin, among a whole horde of others less famous but no less shameless. Back then only misguided white audiences were likely to dance to such church music as *When the Saints Go Marching In* without any sense of transgression.

In the old days to play church music as dance music used to be condemned as a sacrilege by church elders and dance-hall patrons alike. There were some exceptions, of course, and some very notable ones at that. There were the now classic renditions of *The Saints* and *Bye and Bye*, for example, by none other than Louis Armstrong himself. But Armstrong, it must be remembered, besides being a genius (to whom nothing is sacred) was also a product of the highly unconventional religious attitude that the existential

Louis Armstrong as Satchmo the Jester was sometimes the source of embarrassment and confusion
among some civil-rights spokesmen and black college
students; but he always counterstated his clowning
with his trumpet, which was never a laughing matter.

Satchmo the Motion Picture Comedian. (Top) One of the Devil's helpers in *Cabin in the Sky*, 1943. (Bottom) Hamming it up on *Skeleton in the Closet* in *Pennies from Heaven*, 1936.

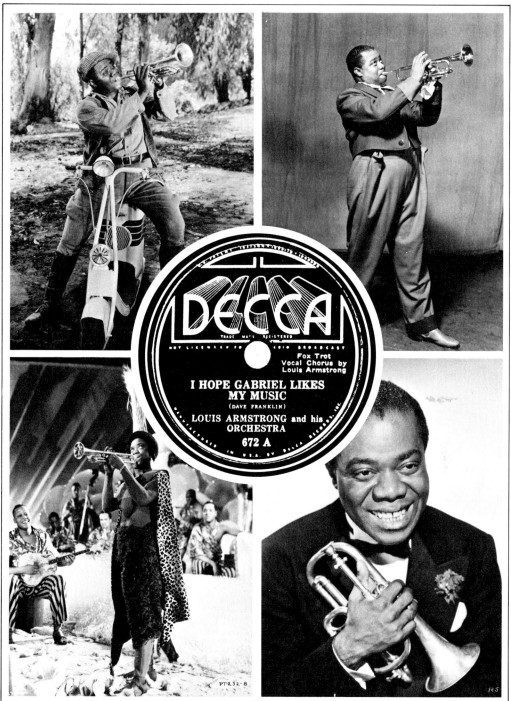

(Top, left) *Going Places,* 1938. (Top, right) As Puck in *A Midsummer Night's Dream.* (Bottom, left) *Rhapsody in Black and Blue,* a Paramount short, 1932. (Bottom, right) As a cornet player and bandleader in *New Orleans,* 1947. (Following spread) The Louis Armstrong that downhome churchfolk were supposed to avoid as if he were the Devil's very own bugle boy.

bodaciousness of New Orleans postcemetery music expresses. Even so, Armstrong almost always legitimized the iconoclasm of his secular use of sacred music with an unmistakable element of parody. Which many outsiders to the downhome church idiom seem to ignore, but which to insiders signals that Armstrong the musician, who sometimes also plays the role of Satchmo the Jester, has now donned the mask of Reverend Dippermouth the Mountebank and is by way of conducting a mock or jivetime church service, so no matter how worked up the musicians become, the deportment and the dance movements of the audience should be governed by the spirit of caricature. Even as are church-sponsored Tom Thumb weddings, in which a cast of children poke fun at the solemnity of religious marriage rites.

Thus Armstrong's use of church music in secular situations was not performed to stimulate the usual dance-hall bumps and grinds, and the same spirit of parody holds true for the mock sermons of Louis Jordan. But such is not always the case with Ray Charles. When he bootlegs *This Little Light of Mine, I'm Goin Let it Shine* into his dance-hall version, *This Little Girl of Mine*, the assumption seems to be that the sacrilege can be nullified by sentimentality; but the effect of doing ballroom and honky-tonk steps to such music would have once struck people of both branches of the idiom as being infinitely more offensive than parody. By comparison, using the name of the Lord in vain would probably have been considered a relatively minor trespass. There is, after all, a world of difference between the way you clap your hands and pat your feet in church and the way people snap their fingers in a ballroom, even when the rhythm, tempo, and even the beat are essentially the same. Once you become a member of the church it is as if you are forbidden to make certain movements; they constitute a violation of a body that has been consecrated to God.

As a matter of fact, a majority of downhome worshipers used to have difficulty reconciling exuberant expression with religious devotion even when it was an indisputable part of a church service. Conventional downhome Baptists and Methodists, as anybody with any firsthand experience will testify, have never been quite at ease about the appropriateness of all the dithyrambic ebullience of the Sanctified or Holy Roller church. Not that they doubt the sincerity of the communicants, whose deportment outside the

Louis Jordan, vocalist, alto player (formerly with the Chick Webb orchestra) and inimitable leader of the Tympany Five, who was at the peak of his international popularity between 1943 and 1953, is best remembered for his renditions of *Caldonia, Is You Is or Is You Ain't My Baby, Knock Me a Kiss, Let the Good Times Roll, Don't Let the Sun Catch You Crying, I'm Gonna Move to the Outskirts of Town, Ain't Nobody Here But Us Chickens, Beware Brother Beware, Choo Choo Ch' Boogie* and *Saturday Night Function*. The element of frolicsome mockery in his verbal delivery is as obvious as is the downhome earthiness represented by the instrumental accompaniment. Incidentally, as should surprise no one, Jordan is completely at home with Armstrong both as a vocalist and as a first-rate instrumentalist on *You Rascal You* and *Life Is So Peculiar,* recorded for Decca in 1950.

church is always very sanctified indeed. But what with all the jam-session-like call-and-response leapfrogging, all the upbeat drumming and on trap drums of all things, all the shimmy-shaking tambourines and free-for-all caper cuttings as if by the numbers, the ragtime overtones of a shindig have always been too much for most conventional witnesses.

As for the blues musician being an agent of affirmation and continuity in the face of adversity, hardly anything could be further from the conventional downhome churchgoer's most fundamental assumptions about the nature of things. The church is not concerned with the affirmation of life as such, which in its view is only a matter of feeble flesh to begin with. The church is committed to the eternal salvation of the soul after death, which is both final and inevitable. Human existence is only a brief sojourn in a vale of trials, troubles, and tribulations to be endured because it is the will of the Creator, whose ways are mysterious.

It is not for man to affirm the will of God, because His will is not something that a mere man can question anyway, no matter how arbitrarily adverse the circumstances. Actually, the only thing that a good church member can affirm is his faith in the Word and God's mercy, because what is forever in doubt is not life, however wretched, but your own worthiness, which is to say, steadfastness in the face of temptation.

The overall solemnity of the services of non-Sanctified downhome churches is entirely in keeping with the fact that more than anything else they are rituals of propitiation, which place primary emphasis not on joyous celebration but on prayer and sacrifice and thanksgiving. Unlike the revelers at the Saturday Night Function, the worshipers attending the Sunday Morning Service are very much concerned with guilt and with seeking forgiveness for their trespasses against the teachings of the Holy Scriptures. Accordingly what each expresses is not affirmation of life as such but rather his determination not to yield to the enticements of the fleshpots of Baal.

But the Saturday Night Function is a ritual of purification and affirmation nonetheless. Not all ceremonial occasions are solemn. Nor are defiance and contestation less fundamental to human well-being than are worship and propitiation. Indeed they seem to be precisely what such indispensably human attributes as courage,

38

James Brown, long-time king of soul musicians. He performs almost as if he were a spellbinding evangelist preacher delivering a shout-getting sermon; and the atmosphere he generates is that of a downhome sanctified church during revival time.

Ray Charles, singer, piano player, and masterful bandleader, is one of the outstanding blues musicians of his generation. As a composer and/or performer of such soul items as *Hallelujah, I Love Her So, Ain't that Love, Talking 'bout You,* and *What Kind of Man Are You,* however, he treats the gospel music of devoted churchgoers as if it were the pop music of Tin Pan Alley.

Mahalia Jackson, 1911-72, one of the greatest gospel singers of all times. In spite of the fact that her mindfulness of the distinction between the sacred and secular modes was such that she never sang blues lyrics and absolutely refused to perform as an entertainer, she achieved a popularity among fans of blues music that was equal to if not greater than that which she already enjoyed in church circles.

dignity, honor, nobility, and heroism are all about. André Malraux might well have been referring to the blues and the function of blues musicians when he described the human condition in terms of ever-impending chaos and declared that each victory of the artist represents a triumph of man over his fate. That he was addressing himself to fundamental implications of heroism should be clear enough.

What the blue devils of gloom and ultimate despair threaten is not the soul or the possibility of everlasting salvation after death, but the quality of everyday life on earth. Thus the most immediate problem of the blues-bedeviled person concerns his ability to cope with even the commonplace. What is at stake is a sense of well-being that is at least strong enough to enable him to meet the basic requirements of the workaday world. Accordingly, in addition to its concern with forthright confrontation and expurgation, the Saturday Night Function also consists of rituals of resilience and perseverance through improvisation in the face of capricious disjuncture.

Still, with all its component rituals that fulfill such pragmatic needs, the Saturday Night Function, unlike the Sunday Morning Service, is also something to be enjoyed solely as an end in itself. After all, beyond the good time (much, if not exactly, the same as with the experience of the work of art) there is mostly only more struggle. Between this Saturday night and the next there is Monday morning and the next work week. In any case, at the Saturday Night Function primary emphasis is placed upon aesthetics not ethics. What is good in such circumstances is the beautiful, without which there can be no good time. What counts is elegance (not only in the music and the dance movement but in the survival technology inherent in the underlying ritual as well).

Not that perhaps most Saturday Night Revelers may not hold the church in traditional reverence at the same time. Many will be present at Sunday Morning Service, sometimes with bloodshot eyes and queasy stomachs, but almost always with breaths de-alcoholized at least somewhat with cinnamon, Juicy Fruit, or peppermint. Nor does it follow that those who never go do not expect a church funeral ceremony. The least that most expect is a few words by a minister at church cemetery.

42

The Blues
as Music

The blues as such are synonymous with low spirits. Blues music is not. With all its so-called blue notes and overtones of sadness, blues music of its very nature and function is nothing if not a form of diversion. With all its preoccupation with the most disturbing aspects of life, it is something contrived specifically to be performed as entertainment. Not only is its express purpose to make people feel good, which is to say in high spirits, but in the process of doing so it is actually expected to generate a disposition that is both elegantly playful and heroic in its nonchalance.

Even when blues lyrics are about the most harrowing anxieties, hardships, and misfortunes (as they so often but by no means always are), blues music is no less appropriate to good-time situations. Even when what the instrumentation represents is the all but literal effect of the most miserable moaning and groaning, the most excruciating screaming and howling, the most pathetic sighing, sobbing, and whimpering, blues music is never presented to more enthusiastic response than at the high point of some festive occasion. Nor is it likely to dampen the spirit of merriment in the least. On the contrary, even when such representations are poorly executed they seldom fail to give the atmosphere an added dimension of down-to-earth sensuality.

That the blues as such are a sore affliction that can lead to total collapse goes without saying. But blues music regardless of its lyrics almost always induces dance movement that is the direct opposite of resignation, retreat, or defeat. Moreover, as anyone

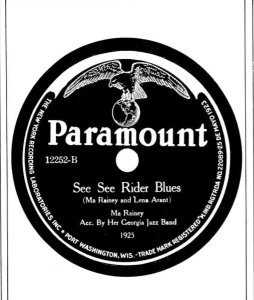

Ma Rainey and her Wildcat Jazz Band of 1923. (Left to right) Gabriel Washington, drums; Al Wynn, trombone; Dave Nelson, trumpet; Eddie Pollack, saxophone; and at the piano, Thomas A. Dorsey, who was later to become a famous composer of gospel songs. Among the well-known instrumentalists who also worked with her on records made between 1924 and 1928 were Louis Armstrong; Joe Smith, cornet; Charlie Green and Kid Ory, trombone; Buster Bailey, clarinet; Don Redman and Coleman Hawkins, saxophone; Tampa Red, guitar; and Fletcher Henderson and Claude Hopkins, piano.

At his peak Jimmie Rushing was easily the most popular attraction in the Count Basie Orchestra that included Buck Clayton, Jo Jones, Walter Page, Dicky Wells, Harry Edison, and the great Lester Young himself.

CLARENCE WILLIAMS
(Exclusive Okeh Artist)

CLARENCE WILLIAMS

And now for some grand baby-grand "blues"! Clarence Williams plays 'em, and folks, that makes 'em 'bout as grand as can be! Clarence writes 'em and sings 'em, too, but his real specialty is taking a "blues" and dressing it up in "rags". We don't mean the kind of rags they put in bags — no, sir! We mean the kind that start your shoes a-shiftin' and your muscles movin'! The Race can boast of some mighty fine piano players but when it comes to teachin' the ivories some new "blues' stuff, Clarence Williams just naturally leads 'em all! He not only plays all by himself, but he also accompanies famous "blues" stars, such as Sara Martin and Eva Taylor, while they sing 'em sweet and pretty. Sara, or Eva, a-singing and Clarence accompanying—you can't beat that for "six-bits", folks!

8067
10 in. .75

MONKEY MAN BLUES Contralto-Baritone Duet with Piano Accomp.
Sara Martin and Clarence Williams
YODELING BLUES Contralto Duet by Sara Martin and Eva Taylor—
Yodel Cornet Obligato by Thomas Morris
Piano Accompaniment by Clarence Williams

4927
10 in. .75

I've Got The Yes! We Have No BANANA BLUES Contralto with Orch.
Eva Taylor With Clarence Williams' Blue Five
OH! DADDY BLUES Contralto-Baritone Duet with Orchestra
Clarence Williams and Eva Taylor With Clar. Williams' Blue Five

4893
10 in. .75

MIXING THE BLUES Piano Solo   Clarence Williams
THE WEARY BLUES Piano Solo   Clarence Williams

THE ORIGINAL RACE RECORDS

CLARA SMITH

"The World's Champion Moaner"

EVERY blues thinks it's full of misery until Clara Smith goes to work on it. Blues, that no ordinary mortal dare tackle, subside into a melodious melody of moans and groans when Clara gets warmed up to her work.

Just look at her smile. What a sight for sore eyes! Listen to her voice. A balm for tired ears! You can hear her voice, and it seems like you can almost get the smile, too, on Columbia New Process Records.

CLARA SMITH

Clara Smith is an Exclusive Columbia Artist

EASE IT . . . . PERCOLATIN' BLUES—*Piano Accompaniments by Lem Fowler*	14202-D	75c
YOU DON'T KNOW WHO'S SHAKIN' YOUR TREE—*Acc'p'd by Her Jazz Babies* CHEATIN' DADDY	14192-D	75c

who has ever shared the fun of any blues-oriented social function should never need to be reminded, the more lowdown, dirty, and mean the music, the more instantaneously and pervasively sensual the dance gestures it engenders. As downright aphrodisiac as blues music so often becomes, however, and as notorious for violence as the reputation of blues-oriented dance-hall records has been over the years, blues-idiom merriment is not marked either by the sensual abandon of the voodoo orgy or by the ecstatic trance of a religious possession. One of its most distinctive features, conversely, is its unique combination of spontaneity, improvisation, and control. Sensual abandon is, like overindulgence in alcohol and drugs, only another kind of disintegration. Blues-idiom dance movement being always a matter of elegance is necessarily a matter of getting oneself together.

Sometimes the Blues Set in a dance program used to be referred to as the one that put the dancers, and in fact the whole event, into the alley, back out in the alley, out in the back alley, or way down in the alley. Because sometimes blues music also used to be said to come from down in the alley. Which meant that it was not only not from the drawing room (and the overextensions and overrefinements thereof), but was of its very essence the sound-equivalent of the unvarnished, or unpainted back-alley actualities of everyday flesh-and-blood experience. Hence, among other things, much of

●

(Preceding page) In recent years, certain self-styled liberal jazz critics have made a special point of registering their disapproval of the use of the term "race records" as an advertising category for blues music in the catalogs of such companies as Columbia, Victor, Decca, Okeh, etc. But since these same writers not only forever intrude the name of Bix Beiderbecke into discussions about such seminal blues-idiom trumpet players as Buddy Bolden, Bunk Johnson, Freddie Keppard, King Oliver, and Louis Armstrong, but also make no outcry whatsoever about the numberless articles that describe Benny Goodman as the King of Swing or the polls which rate Woody Herman and Stan Kenton over Duke Ellington and Count Basie, their motives are open to some question. Are they truly concerned about the symbolic segregation expressed by the term "race records," or are they aiming at a redefinition of blues music that will legitimize the idiomatic authenticity of certain white musicians, whose very accents indicate that they are *not* native to the idiom but who nonetheless enjoy reputations (and earnings) as great performers? The fact remains—oblivious as certain critics may be to it—that in the black press of the 1920s the most prominent Negro leaders and spokesmen referred to themselves as race spokesmen and race leaders. The period of the race catalogs was also the decade of the so-called revolution in race consciousness known as the Harlem Renaissance, when the term "race"—as in race man, race brother and sister, race-educator, race interests, credit to the race, etc.—was synonymous with group self-pride among U.S. Negroes, much as the term "black" came to be used in the decade of the 1960s. In any case, the indignation over the race terminology as applied to records has been misguided at best. The only real victims here were those Negro recording firms such as Black Swan which originated race records—only to be put out of business by Columbia, Decca, Okeh, and Victor.

the onomatopoeia of the workaday world and at least some of the dirty tones and raggy overtones of the riffraff and the rabble.

Which by the same token is also why the Blues Set is sometimes said to be the one that gets things back down to the so-called nitty gritty, which is to say back down from the cloudlike realms of abstraction and fantasy to the bluesteel and rawhide textures of the elemental facts of the everyday struggle for existence. As a result of which the dancers (who were sometimes said to have been put in the groove) were normally expected to respond not with uneasiness and gestures of fear and trembling but with warm person-to-person intimacy that was both robust and delicate.

In short, the situation for which the blues as such are synonymous is always at least somewhat regrettable if not utterly wretched and grievous. But as preoccupied with human vulnerability as so many of its memorable lyrics have always been, and as suggestive of pain as some of its instrumentation sometimes seems to be, blues music can hardly be said to be synonymous with lamentation and commiseration. Not when the atmosphere of earthiness and the disposition to positive action it engenders are considered. And besides, sometimes the lyrics mock and signify even as they pretend to weep, and as all the finger snapping, foot tapping, and hip cocking indicate, the instrumentation may be far less concerned with agony than with ecstasy.

Which, incidentally, should make it easy enough to distinguish between blues music on the one hand and the secularized gospel music known as soul music and the rhythm-and-folk blues-oriented hillbilly music known as rock music (erstwhile ofay rock-and-roll or rockabilly) on the other. Both soul and rock make free use of idiomatic devices borrowed from blues musicians, but the so-called funky atmosphere they generate is charged with sentimentality rather than earthiness. Also, soul and rock almost always place primary emphasis on a one-dimensional earnestness that all too easily deteriorates into a whining self-pity or a highly amplified tantrum of banging and crashing and screaming and stamping that obviously has far more to do with the intensification of a mood of despair than with getting rid of any demons of gloom.

Not that there is no such thing as sorrowful blues music. But not so much as many people seem to think. Not that there have not always been some blues musicians trying to earn a living by mak-

51

Cordially Yours
Blind Lemon Jefferson

Blind Lemon Jefferson was widely known, especially throughout the South, because of his record-ings. He appeared in person mainly on street corners, at picnics, in honky-tonks, and at various private and semi-private socials including house-rent parties on Chicago's South Side.

Bessie Smith in 1924, the year she recorded *Ticket Agent, Ease Your Window Down, Bo'weevil Blues, Work House Blues, Louisiana Low Down Blues,* and *Hateful Blues.*

ing wretchedness a public feature. But the blind musician on the corner with his tin cup has never been the typical blues musician. Unlike Ma Rainey, Bessie Smith, Jimmy Rushing, and Big Joe Turner, whose acts were always a part if not the high point of the main event, he is at best only a sobering sideshow. On the other hand, a blind musician putting the dancers in a lowdown back-alley groove at a Saturday Night Function needs no tin cup.

Even those people who sing, play, dance to, or just listen to blues music mostly because they feel blue seem much less likely to do so in self-commiseration than because it helps them get rid of the blues. But even so, most people listen to blues music for the simple fact that it always makes them feel good. And they are just as likely to listen and dance to it when they already feel very good, because it always makes them feel even better. As for those who sing and play it, they do so not to publicize their most intimate secrets and most personal embarrassments but because Music is their profession and blues music is an idiom for which they feel they have some aesthetic affinity and technical competence. Nor are they likely to have chosen music in the first place because of some personal calamity which they feel compelled to spend the rest of their lives publishing abroad, but rather because their admiration for some older musician led to emulation. Bessie Smith, for example, owes much more to Ma Rainey than to hard luck, and she also owes not a little to the good luck that began with being born with a voice the magnificence of which, like that of Louis Armstrong's trumpet and Duke Ellington's orchestrations, no amount of adversity has yet produced in anybody else.

Blues Music as Such

Definitions of blues music in most standard American dictionaries confuse it with the blues as such. They also leave the impression that what it represents is the expression of sadness. Not one characterizes it as good-time music. Nor is there any reference whatsoever to its use as dance music. Moreover, primary emphasis is always placed on its vocal aspects, and no mention at all is made of the fact that over the years it has come to be dominated by dance-hall-oriented instrumentalists to a far greater extent than by singers.

According to the third edition of *Webster's New International Dictionary*, blues music is "a song sung or composed in a style originating among American Negroes, characterized typically by use of three-line stanzas in which the words of the second line repeat the first, expressing a mood of longing or melancholy, and marked by a continual occurrence of blue notes in melody and harmony." Which not only suggests that musicians pray the blues instead of playing them, but also limits the mood to melancholy and longing. Bessie Smith's recording of *Florida Bound Blues* which begins, "Goodbye, North; Hello, South . . ." is tinged with melancholy to be sure, but what it expresses in the main is determination (to get back down South to a good place) and in the process it becomes a paean for a good man. Determination is also stronger than the melancholy strains of her *One and Two Blues*. The regret is unmistakable, but as in *The Golden Rule*, *Hard Driving Papa*, and *Worn Out Papa*, the point is to get *him* told off—as the point in Jimmy Rushing's (and Count Basie's) *Goin' to Chicago* (Columbia G31224) is to get *her* told.

57

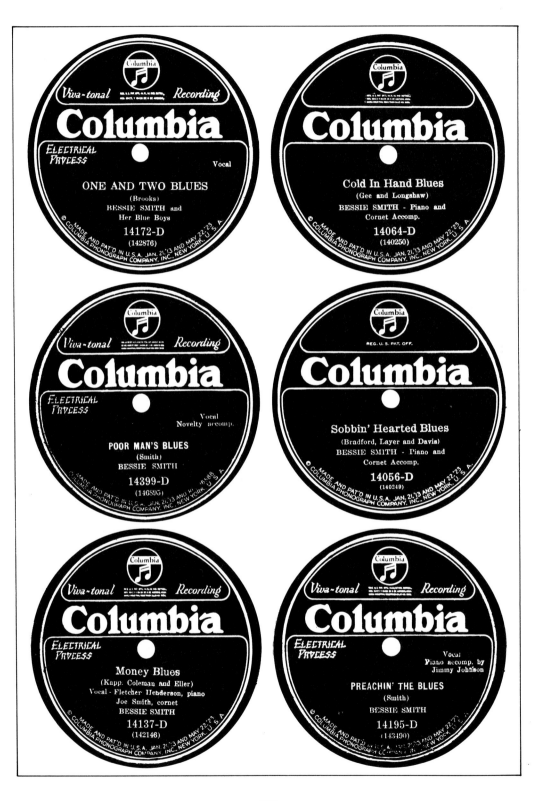

58

The most magnificent blues diva of them all, as she is remembered by downhome Saturday Night Revelers and Sunday Morning Worshipers alike.

Hard Driving Papa
(Brooks)
Vocal - Fletcher Henderson, piano
Joe Smith, cornet
BESSIE SMITH
14137-D
(142148)

The entry in *Webster's* also fails to take into account such un-disputed classics of the idiom as Louis Armstrong's renditions of *The Memphis Blues* and *Beale Street Blues*, in which the mood is joyous and in which instead of melancholy and longing there is low gravy mellowness. Thus Armstrong's version of *The St. Louis Blues* (RCA Victor LPM-2971) would also be precluded. The melody would qualify and so would the lyrics in part, but the actual mood of the performance in question (which is determined by the up-tempo beat plus the riff-style call-and-response choruses) would not.

The clues provided by *Webster's Collegiate*, the much more widely consulted desk-size abridgement of *Webster's New International* are of very little practical use. If blues music is, as it states, a type of song written in a characteristic key with melancholy lyrics and syncopated rhythms, then neither W. C. Handy's *The Memphis Blues* (said to be the first blues ever copyrighted) nor his *Aunt Hagar's Blues* qualifies. Neither has melancholy lyrics. (Incidentally, although Aunt Hagar herself is represented as describing blues music as melancholy, she is also quoted as saying "When my feet say dance, I just can't refuse—When I hear that melody they call the Blues.")

The *American College Dictionary* reports that blues music is melancholy in character and usually performed in slow tempo. But while this applies to any number of other kinds of music, including the spirituals, it does not apply to such standard Kansas City blues compositions as Pete Johnson's *Roll Em, Pete* or Count Basie's *Sent for You Yesterday*, which are usually played in up-tempo.

Funk and Wagnall's Encyclopedic Dictionary echoes standard confusion of blues music with the blues as such, as does the *World Book Dictionary*, which implies that blues music is any composition played in a slow jazz rhythm as a lamentation!

The relatively new *American Heritage Dictionary* gives mis-representations and restrictions that are as old as the rest: "A style of jazz evolved from southern American Negro secular songs and usually distinguished ·by slow tempos and flatted thirds and sevenths." Which again places too much emphasis upon slowness. Some blues music is most effective in a slow tempo. Some is best in a moderate tempo. Some should always be played in up-tempo. Many are no less effective in one as in another. However, it is hard

W. C. Handy

and his "Blues" — COVARRUBIAS

"ST LOUIS BLUES"   "WALL STREET BLUES"
"YELLOW DOG BLUES"   "AUNT AGAR'S BLUES"
"HESITATING BLUES"   "GOLDEN BROWN BLUES"
"BEALE STREET BLUES"   "JOE TURNER BLUES"
"LOVELESS LOVE BLUES"   "MEMPHIS BLUES"

Promotion copy sometimes represented W. C. Handy as the "Father of the Blues" and sometimes as the "Originator of the Blues." Handy's own account does not back such a claim—although in fact he claimed credit for writing the first blues to be published, which he clearly pointed out was based on a form already in existence and already known as the blues. Handy did pioneer not only in the composition but in the publication of blues scores for professional musicians.

to imagine either of the following traditional verses performed in anything except up-tempo:

> Well the blues jumped the rabbit and run him for a solid mile
> Said the blues jumped the rabbit and run him for a solid mile
> Till the rabbit laid down and cried like a little baby chile.

> What makes my grandma love my grandpa so
> S'what makes old grandma love old grandpa so
> W' he can still hoochie coochie like he did fifty years ago!

(Incidentally instruments can shout such stanzas to an even greater effect than voices.)

Grove's *Dictionary of Music and Musicians* (5th edition, 1960) is generally considered by professionals and students alike to be a long-established and highly authoritative standard reference in the field of music. Yet its discussion of the blues as music, written by Hugues Panassié, one of the earliest critical experts in the field, contains perhaps as much confusion and nonsense as facts and insights:

> The origin of the blues is unknown; they are probably of remote African provenance, but the form in which we know them today is predominantly American. They bear, in fact, very definitely the stigma of the yoke of slavery to which the black races were subjected in the U.S.A., as may be gathered from the note of pathos which makes them emotionally as disturbing as any of the world's music. Yet when Negroes sing their blues it is not in order to give in to sadness, but rather to find relief from it. That is why the blues are never sentimental, in the pejorative sense of the term, but on the contrary full of vitality that shows no mere resignation in the American Negro, but a protest against the sad lot that was inflicted upon him.
>
> From the technical point of view the blues are short pieces twelve bars in length based on an invarying harmonic sequence. The difference between two blues lies exclusively in the melody superimposed on the harmonies—and even that is often the same—in the words, and particularly, in each singer's individual performance.
>
> The outstanding melodic characteristic of the blues, and that of the harmony resulting from the tunes, is its tendency to flatten certain notes of the scale by a semitone, which have for that reason been called "blue notes."

It is far more accurate to say that some of the most distinctive *elements* of blues music were derived from the music of *some* of the West African ancestors of U.S. Negroes than it is to imply, however obliquely, that the blues idiom itself ever existed anywhere on the continent of Africa. Nor should it be forgotten that elements quite as essential and no more dispensable were derived from the music of some of the European ancestors of U.S. Negroes.

The point, however, is that the blues idiom, whatever the source or sources of its components, is native to the United States. It is a synthesis of African and European elements, the product of an Afro-American sensibility in an American mainland situation. There is no evidence, for example, that an African musical sensibility interacting with an Italian, German, French, British, or Hungarian musical sensibility results in anything like blues music. The synthesis of European and African musical elements in the West Indies, the Caribbean, and in continental Latin America produced calypso, rhumba, the tango, the conga, mambo, and so on, but not the blues and not ragtime, and not that extension, elaboration, and refinement of blues-break riffing and improvisation which came to be known as jazz.

In point of historical fact, the use of the word *blue* (which is European to begin with) to connote an emotional state or circumstance has much more to do with light-skinned people than with dark-skinned people. Figures of speech, after all, are always likely to have been derived from concrete experience. In any event, not only is it natural for people of European pigmentation to think of themselves as literally changing colors as a result of an emotional state, but English lexicographers have found records that show that the phrase "to look blue," meaning to suffer anxiety, fear, discomfort, and low spirits, was in currency as long ago as 1550. (Incidentally, one Middle English form of the word was bla, which survives in the word *blae*, sometimes spelled *blah* and thought to be a colloquialism for feeling dull, bored, dispirited, but which in Middle English already referred to looking as well as feeling livid or leaden.)

On the other hand it would seem extremely unlikely that the African ancestors of U.S. Negro blues musicians were any more inclined to describe themselves as turning blue with sorrow than to say that their faces were red with embarrassment or excitement, or

63

that they were turning green with envy. Thus the chances were that blues-oriented Afro-Americans acquired both the word and its special connotation from their Euro-American ancestors. English usage of the term blue devils to designate baleful demons has been traced back as far as 1616. Its figurative use as a metaphor for depression of spirits has been traced as far back as 1787, and its plural use as a name for apparitions seen or experienced during delirium tremens has been in use since 1822.

American usage of the blues as a term for depressed spirits, despondency, and melancholy dates, according to *The Dictionary of American English on Historical Principles*, at least as far back as 1807, when Washington Irving used the following sentence in *Salamagundi XI*: "He concluded his harangue with a sigh, and I saw that he was still under the influence of a whole legion of the blues." And no less of a national figure than Thomas Jefferson is on record as having written in 1810: "We have something of the blue devils at times."

Other instances have been documented by the *Dictionary of American English* as follows: 1820, *Western Carolinean*, 18 July, "The fact is he was but recently convalescent from a severe spell of the blues"; 1837, *Southern Literary Messenger III*, 387, "I shall have a fit of the blues if I stay here"; 1850, N. Kingsley *Diary*, 143, "Some are beginning to get the blues on most horribly"; 1866, Gregg, *Life in the Army*, "It was well for me that day that I was able to look on the brightest side of the case and avoid a severe attack of the blues"; 1871, *Scribner's Monthly* I, 489, "The Silence alone is enough to give a well man the blues"; 1883, *Harper's Magazine*, Dec., 55, "Come to me when you have the blues."

All of which suggests that blues music bears a vernacular relationship to the blues that is much if not very nearly the same as that which the spirituals bear to the Christianity of frontier America. Musicologists have indeed traced numerous rhythmic, structural, and sonic elements of the spirituals to African sources, but the fact remains that the spirituals as a specific musical idiom are both indigenous and peculiar to the religious experience of Africans transplanted to the United States. They are a product of the interaction of certain elements derived from African religious and musical sensibilities with European-derived music and religion. But this interaction only took place in the United States. Not in Africa, for all the Africans converted by European missionaries; and not in Europe, and not even in the Caribbean and Latin American countries.

Likewise, the actual historical as well as geographic circumstances, and consequently the conceptual framework in terms of which the blues as such are first perceived, defined, and then responded to by musicians and dancers is not West African, nor is it European. Nor Euro-African. It is Afro-U.S. However many demons there might have been in ancestral West Africa and however many of them may have been some ominous shade of blue, the specific rituals—if any—they gave rise to were likely to be far more closely related to voodoo ceremonies than to the Saturday Night Function. The underlying dance-beat dislosition involved is obviously West African in origin, and so are the definitive stylistic elements that give the incantation and percussion—which is to say, blues music—its special idiomatic character. But even so the blues seem to have been imported to the United States from Europe, along with the Christian conception of God and the angels of Heaven and the Devil and the imps of Hell.

●

Hugues Panassié's description of blues music as "bearing very definitely the stigma of the yoke of slavery—as may be gathered from the note of pathos . . ." is highly questionable to say the least. To most musicologists the so-called note of pathos is largely a matter of African-derived quarter-tone or blue notes, which is to say, a matter of convention and tradition predating the importation of black slaves to the United States. Moreover, the subject matter and imagery of blues lyrics are usually nothing if not concrete and specific, and not unlike the subject matter and imagery of lyric poetry in general, they are much more preoccupied with love affairs than with such political issues as liberty, equality, and justice.

What with all the references in the spirituals to The House of Bondage, The Walls of Jericho, The Lion's Den, The Fiery Furnace, Deliverance from Old King Pharaoh, The Wilderness, The Valley of the Shadow, The Rainbow Sign, and The Promised Land, it is easy enough to associate their deeply moving sonorities with slavery and political oppression. Indeed, even the most

65

metaphysical concerns of the spirituals often readily lend themselves to immediate political interpretation and application. Also, such is the intrinsically moral orientation of the imagery of the spirituals that no great violence is done to the essential poetic statement when references to the spiritual predicament of man are seen as reflecting his earthly plight.

But even when blues lyrics address themselves directly to negative economic, political, and judiciary circumstances, far more often than not, the main emphasis is likely to be placed on the victim's love life. The pseudo-folk lyrics currently so dear to the hearts of avant-garde night-club patrons and self-styled revolutionary revelers blame the crooked judge, but traditional folk lyrics are about the damage to a love affair. The source of the trouble that brings on the blue tormentors being addressed by Bessie Smith in *Jailhouse Blues, Workhouse Blues, House Rent Blues, Money Blues, Hard Times Blues,* and *Backwater Blues* is not perceived as the political system as such but rather almost always as some unfaithful lover. In fact in the 160 available recordings of Bessie Smith (Columbia five-album set, GP33, G30126, G30450, G30818, G31093), a few notable exceptions such as *Washwoman's Blues* and *Poor Man's Blues* notwithstanding, the preoccupation is clearly not at all with hard workmasters, cruel sheriffs, biased prosecutors, juries, and judges, but with the careless love of aggravating papas, sweet mistreaters, dirty nogooders, and spider men. Old Pharaoh in the spirituals may often stand for Ole Marster as well as the ruler of a sinful and oppressive nation; and Egyptland is often the U.S. South as well as the mundane world. But the man who imprisons the woman body-and-soul in Bessie Smith's lyrics is neither sheriff nor warden. He is the slow and easy but sometimes heartless lover.

In any case, Panassié's political emphasis is not borne out by any outstanding internal evidence of political consciousness. Therefore his characterization of blues music as "a protest against the sad lot that was inflicted on him [i.e., U.S. Negroes]" is gratuitous for all its unquestionably good intentions.

As a matter of fact, much goes to show that in the world as represented by most traditional blues lyrics, it is usually as if the political system were simply another elemental phenomenon, as much a part of the nature of things as were the inscrutable forces

Bessie Smith in 1923, the year she made her first recordings, including *Gulf Coast Blues, Aggravatin Papa, Baby Won't You Please Come Home,* with Clarence Williams on piano; *Jail House Blues,* with Jasper Johns on piano; and *Any Woman's Blues,* with Fletcher Henderson on piano. Between 1912 and 1922 she worked in theaters such as Bailey's 81 in Atlanta, toured the South with such groups as the Florida Blossoms and Silas Green, and was already a vaudeville prima donna with a considerable following before her first records were released. By the end of 1923 her popularity was that of a superstar.

personified by the Gods of Mount Olympus, which also suggests the possibility that the source of any overtone of pathos that may be heard is likely to be more existential or even metaphysical than political. Nor is such an eventuality in the least inconsistent with charges made by church elders against blues music when they accuse it of being good-time music. The overtones they hear are mostly of frivolity.

Not that blues music is without fundamental as well as immediate political significance and applicability. But the nature of its political dimension is not always as obvious as some promoters of folk-music-as-social-commentary seem to believe. The political implication is inherent in the attitude toward experience that generates the blues-music counterstatement in the first place. It is the disposition to persevere (based on a tragic, or, better still, an epic sense of life) that blues music at its best not only embodies but stylizes, extends, elaborates, and refines into art. And, incidentally, such is the ambiguity of artistic statement that there is no need to choose between the personal implication and the social, except as the occasion requires.

As for the note of pathos that Panassié finds to be as moving as that of any other music in the world, the element of downright sadness, forlornness, bitter deprivation, and raw anguish is by all odds a far greater characteristic of the folk music of white southerners than of the downhome honky-tonk Saturday Night Function and ballroom. When a hillbilly musician or country-and-western musician plays or sings a lament, the music is likely to reinforce the mood of melancholy and longing, but in the performance of a blues ballad the chances are that even the most solemn words of a dirge will not only be counterstated by the mood of earthy well-being stimulated by the beat but may even be mocked by the jazziness of the instrumentation.

As imprecisely as the words of so many blues lyrics are treated in actual performance, even by the most celebrated vocalists, beginning with Ma Rainey and Bessie Smith, and including Louis Armstrong, Jimmy Rushing, and Big Joe Turner, they provide the most specific clues to the historical source of the blues predicament to which they address themselves. What blues instrumentation in fact does, often in direct contrast to the words, is define the nature of the response to the blues situation at hand, whatever the source.

Accordingly, more often than not, even as the words of the lyrics recount a tale of woe, the instrumentation may mock, shout defiance, or voice resolution and determination.

Panassié, however, as the entry in Grove's *Dictionary* also goes on to show, is by no means unaware of the affirmative thrust of blues music. Having overstated the historical implications of what he calls the note of pathos, he states in the very next sentence that when Negroes play their blues it is not to give way to sadness, but rather to find relief from it, which he says is "why the blues are never sentimental in the pejorative sense." In his book *The Real Jazz* he puts it somewhat differently:

> It has been stated that the blues were a cry of the black man's soul under the oppression of the whites. Hence the plaintive quality, the often hopeless accent. But let us make no mistake; when a Negro sings the blues it is not to give way to sadness, it is rather to free himself of it. He has far too much optimism and too vivid a sense of life to permit himself to do otherwise. That is why the blues, in spite of their nostalgic mood, have nothing to do with whining—but rather express a confidence, a tonic sense of vitality. The Negro has no time for that sentimental, languorous tone which is the scourge of so much music . . . . Furthermore when the blues are sung in rapid rather than slow time they can assume an even joyful note.[!]

Perhaps it is overemphasis based on assumptions that are too specifically political that prevent some commentators from realizing that it may be much more to the point to speak rather of a difference of conventions between blues and hillbilly music than to characterize the latter, if only by implication, as bearing no stigma of the yoke of slavery—or as bearing a greater stigma of something else. The correlation of plaintive musical overtones with political status is not likely to be very clearcut in either case.

But then the term *stigma* can hardly do justice to the complex heritage of the experience of slavery in the United States anyway. Much is forever being made of the deleterious effects of slavery on the generations of black Americans that followed. But for some curious reason, nothing at all is ever made of the possibility that the legacy left by the enslaved ancestors of blues-oriented contemporary U.S. Negroes includes a disposition to confront the most unpromising circumstances and make the most of what little there is to go on, regardless of the odds—and not without finding delight in the process or forgetting mortality at the height of ecstasy. Still there is a lot of admittedly infectious exuberance, elegance and nonsense to be accounted for.

●

The entry in *A Dictionary of Americanisms on Historical Principles*, which defines blues music as "a type of mournful, haunting Negro folk song adapted and often burlesqued for use in music halls, vaudeville shows, etc.," includes two fundamental clues omitted by other standard references, only to misinterpret them and end up with the same old confusion and exclusions. But once the mood has been limited to haunting mournfulness and the level of execution to that of folk (which is to say nonprofessional or semiprofessional if not amateur) expression, it is no doubt easy enough to preclude burlesque or ridicule as perfectly normal elements of blues-idiom statement, and to imply that the music hall and the vaudeville stage are not its natural setting. Eliminated by doing so, however, are Ma Rainey, Bessie, Clara, Mamie, and Trixie Smith, Ida Cox, Jelly Roll Morton, Louis Armstrong to name a few, the best of whose work often contained elements of burlesque, mockery, and derision, and was nothing if not music hall and vaudeville along with whatever else it was.

The vaudeville circuit was as natural to Ma Rainey, the Smith queens, and Louis Armstrong as the street corner and the cheap honky-tonk were to Blind Lemon Jefferson and Robert Johnson. Nor was their music a special adaptation of folk expression. It was rather a perfectly natural historical development. It was an extension, elaboration, and refinement that was no mere embellishment but an evolution altogether consistent with the relative sophistication of the musicians involved.

That blues music began as folk expression goes without saying. Nor have the original folk-type blues musicians ever gone out of existence. But in point of historical fact, once W. C. Handy had arranged, scored and published *The Memphis Blues* (1912), *The St. Louis Blues* and *Yellow Dog Blues* (1914) and *Beale Street Blues* (1916), it was no longer possible to restrict blues music to the category of folk expression. Certainly there was nothing provincial about the musicians who were providing the instrumentation for Bessie Smith by the early 1920s when her now classic repertory was being established as a nationwide phenomenon (via phono-

70

(Top) Street-corner and honky-tonk folk music. (Bottom) Dance-hall compositions for professional musicians.

MAMIE SMITH
(Exclusive Okeh Artist)

MAMIE SMITH

The "Blue Book of Blues" starts right here, folks! And a right smart start it gets, too, with these "blues" by Mamie Smith — the pretty little high-brown who has the honor of being the first woman of the Race to sing a "blues" and, as an exclusive OKeh artist, the first one to make a real Race record. There's mighty dog-gone few "blues" lovers who have not heard Mamie's unbeatable style of singing. Her sensational vaudeville tours, musical comedy engagements and popular OKeh records have made her nationally famous as the "Colored Queen of Syncopation". Mamie sure serves her stuff "hot" — and man, we're showing you below, her complete menu!

4960 { **MISTREATIN' DADDY BLUES** Contralto Solo, With Piano Accomp.
10 in. .75 { **Mamie Smith**
PLAIN OLD BLUES Contralto Solo With Piano Accomp.   **Mamie Smith**

4935 { **GOOD LOOKING PAPA** Contralto Solo, Piano Accomp. by Clarence
Williams   **Mamie Smith**
10 in. .75 { **YOU CAN'T DO WHAT MY LAST MAN DID** Contralto Solo, Piano
Accomp.   **Mamie Smith**

4926 { **KANSAS CITY MAN BLUES** Contralto Solo, Accompanied by Harlem
Trio   **Mamie Smith**
10 in. .75 { **LADY LUCK BLUES** Contralto Solo, Accompanied by Harlem Trio
Mamie Smith

THE ORIGINAL RACE RECORDS

Definitions of blues music in standard dictionaries place primary emphases on lamentation, longing, and slow tempo. But advertisements from the recording companies, created to appeal to the listener's sense of style, almost always represented top performers in regal terms—suggestive not of sadness but of authority and glamor. (Opposite) A page from the Okeh catalogue of 1923.

graph records to a great extent). Clarence Williams, Fletcher Henderson, James P. Johnson, Louis Armstrong, Joe Smith, Buster Bailey, Coleman Hawkins, Charlie Green, and the rest were anything but folk performers. They were professionals with no less talent and authenticity for all the technical facility, range, and control at their command.

The entry on blues music in the *Standard Dictionary of Folklore, Mythology, and Legend* describes the poetry of the blues as the "tender, ironic, bitter, humorous, or typical expression of a deprived people"; and then goes on to catalogue the subject matter of the blues as careless love, the woman who has lost her man, the no-good woman a man can't forget, the longing to go north with train whistles in the night, floods, cyclones, jails, chain gangs, levee camps, lonesome roads, back alleys, and barrelhouses. It is a source of some wonder to find the barrelhouse, a place of merriment if there ever was one, included in a catalogue of examples of deprivation. Elsewhere the *Standard Dictionary of Folklore, Mythology, and Legend* describes it with casual condescension as cheap: "A cheap saloon of the period of about 1900 during which jazz developed, in which customers could fill their own glasses from a cask, the drip from the spigot falling into a 'gutbucket' on the floor." Not all barrelhouses were cheap, though none were very swanky. Not all permitted customers to serve themselves: but the barrel and the gutbucket are touchstones of nostalgia, not regret. The term, the entry also goes on to say, "is applied to the kind of music played in such places and especially to the rough, 'dirty' timbre of instrumental tone characteristic of this early jazz." But barrelhousing has more to do with dance rhythm than with timbre, and is associated mostly with the piano. A dirty tone on a trumpet or clarinet, for instance, is not referred to as barrel-house.

Overemphasis on the sociopolitical is evident again in such remarks as, "Singing the blues is one way to say what would not be tolerated in speech. Chain gang bosses, for instance, will ignore comment in song about the work, the food, the misery, of the prisoners, that would bring swift reprisal if spoken, so long as the picks and hammers keep swinging to the music, the words don't matter, except to those who sing them."

Of much more practical use are such observations as follow:

Musically, the blues are distinguished by an 8 or 12 bar structure (16 and 20 bars in later stages), by a strongly antiphonal quality, by syncopation and by polyrhythm characteristic of Negro music, by simple harmonic progressions, and by a slight flatting of the third and seventh intervals of the scale, these latter are known as "blue notes". Singers make use of subtle variations in pitch and rhythm, portamento, and a wide range of tone coloration. Certain passages may be hummed or rendered in nonsense syllables called "scat." Instrumental accompaniment (by guitar, piano, or various combinations) improvises melodic and rhythmic patterns to the singer's lead or around a solo instrument, and achieves enormous tonal variety by the use of vibrato, mutes, and ordinarily non-musical instruments such as washboards, jugs, etc.

Also to the point are the following observations on the blues lyric:

The stanza consists typically of a statement repeated one or more times, sometimes with slight variations and a gnomic comment or response. This construction, both in the words and in the music that is molded to them, relates to earlier Negro styles of religious and work singing, with their narrative call lines and responses, and back to African singing. The "punch" lines in their frequently proverbial form, hark back to widespread African use of proverbs in song and story, and the whole song may be of a double-meaning, allusive character close to the African songs of allusion and derision.

●

The Random House Dictionary of the English Language defines blues music as "a song of American Negro origin, that is marked by the frequent occurrence of blue notes, and that takes the basic form, customarily improvised upon in performance, of a 12-bar chorus consisting of a 3-line stanza with the second line repeating the first. . . . the genre consisting of such songs." Thus it does not make the usual mistake of confusing blues music with blues as such. But it is misleading nevertheless. Blues music is always an artful combination of incantation and percussion. It is not always song in the conventional sense of the word. Sometimes if not most times the incantation is instrumental, and while it is true that blues instrumentation is derived from voice extension, it is equally true that much vocalization is now derived from instrumentation.

In all events, defining blues music as song not only gives the lyrics more emphasis than is warranted by the way they are used

75

in actual performance, but also contributes the assumption implicit in those misdefinitions which confuse the music with the blues as such in the first place: that what is said is more important than the way it is said. It is not. The truth is that when a singer likes the tune he is likely to proceed as if any words will do. Moreover much goes to show that only a very few of the millions of devoted admirers of Ma Rainey, Bessie Smith, Jimmy Rushing, and Big Joe Turner, for instance, can actually understand more than half the words of their lyrics as sung, not to mention the idiomatic imagery and references. Perhaps many respond to what they wish to think is being said rather than to the statement the composer wrote, but even so the chances are that most of their goose pimples and all of their finger snapping and foot tapping are produced by the sound far more often than by the meanings of the words.

Singing
the Blues

As compelling as so many blues lyrics so often are, and for all the apt phrases, insightful folksay, and striking imagery that blues singers have added to the national lore, the definitive element of a blues statement is not verbal. Words as such, however well chosen, are secondary to the music. What counts for most is not verbal precision (which is not to say vocal precision) but musical precision, or perhaps better still, musical nuance. Even the most casual survey of the recordings of Ma Rainey, Bessie Smith, Louis Armstrong, Jimmy Rushing and Big Joe Turner, to say nothing of Blind Lemon Jefferson, Leadbelly, and Robert Johnson, will show that it is not at all unusual for blues lyrics of the very highest poetic quality to be mumbled, hummed, and even garbled by the outstanding performers of the idiom.

Folklore-oriented social historians (sometimes also known as compilers of oral history) and tone-deaf lexicographers—not blues musicians and Saturday night revelers—seem most inclined to ascribe primary significance to the literal content of blues lyrics. Blues singers almost always seem to be much more preoccupied with vocal subtleties than with rendering the lyrics as written. Not that any singer is ever likely to be in the least unmindful of the power of eloquence. After all, some of the blues singer's lines are likely to be even more widely quoted than the holy gospel according to the reigning evangelical spellbinders.

But all the same, the blues singer's primary concern with words is not as a conventional means of coherent communication. So long as the vocalist hits the desired notes, the essential message is not

Seldom have singers performed all of the three verses and five choruses of the lyrics that Handy wrote for the original *St. Louis Blues*. The second chorus lines about loving that man like a schoolboy loves his pie and like a Kentucky Colonel loves his mint and rye (usually sung as rock and rye) are still familiar to the general public, but hardly anybody ever takes off on the stovepipe brown of the third verse or the black-headed gal of the third chorus anymore—or the blond and the red-head in the fourth chorus, or the ashes and dust and jazzing in the fifth.

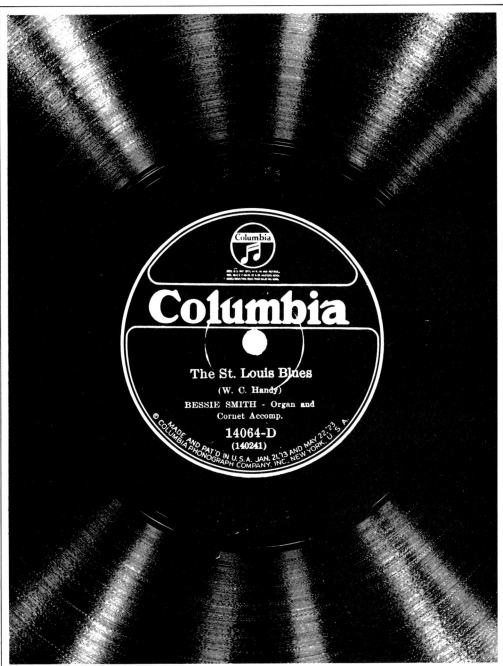

Bessie Smith's classic rendition consists of only the first verse and chorus of the original *St. Louis Blues*. But she makes several alterations in the lyrics even so. Most notably she changes "pack my *trunk* and make my git-away" to "pack my *grip*" (*i.e.*, suitcase) which suggests that she intends to travel considerably lighter than Handy seems to have had in mind. Incidentally, although the words, the slow tempo, and the ever so sorrowful harmonium accompaniment are all geared to lamentation, what her great and irrepressibly earthy voice expresses is a determination that is as undaunted as that of an empress of the earth itself.

greatly impaired by mispronunciation, sloppy syntax, or even misquotation. The chances are that when in her recording of *Yellow Dog Blues*, Bessie Smith misquotes "Letters come from down in 'Bam/and everywhere that Uncle Sam has even rural delivery!/" as "And everywhere that Uncle Sam is the ruler of delivery/" the change if noted was not in the least disturbing to her listeners.

And yet the substitution substantially alters the image. Handy's was a topical reference to U.S. R.F.D. (rural free delivery), a then recent phenomenon, still in process of development in 1914. The change has no less topical overtones, but of post–World War I U.S. military might. In 1925, the time of Bessie's record, newspaper reports of U.S. Marine operations in the Caribbean made Uncle Sam seem the ruler of many far-flung places. The point, however, is that the musical authority with which she hits "and everywhere that Uncle Sam is the RULER of de . . ." overrides the distortion of the original fact. (She hits it, by the way, with exactly the same authority as a first-bench Amen Corner church sister singing: "and everywhere that God Almighty is the RULER.") She also sings "Dear Sue: Your easy rider struck this burg today/on a southbound rattler *beside* the Pullman car/" where as Handy had written: "on a southbound rattler, side door Pullman car," which is a slangy reference to riding in an empty boxcar. But once again, who really cared? Because, as the scat vocal has always illustrated beyond doubt, when the singer sounds good enough the words don't have to make any sense at all.

The concrete information contained in a blues lyric as performed is likely to be largely incidental. The essential message is usually conveyed by the music, whether vocal or instrumental. Thus regardless of how scrupulously accurate the singer's rendition of even the most powerful lyrics, that verbal statement can be contradicted and in effect canceled by any musical counterstatement. If the lyric laments but the music mocks, the statement is not one of lamentation but of mockery. If the words are negative yet the music either up-tempo or even medium or slow but earthy, the tidings are not sad but glad withal. Even when the tempo is drag-time, it is far more likely to be sensual than funereal. The words may bemoan the loss of a lover, but if the singer is also involved with such choreographic gestures as finger popping, shoulder rocking, and hip swinging all the while, the statement can

82

If blues lyrics in themselves accounted for as much as most standard dictionary definitions so obviously take for granted, the effect they create would be quite different from what it is in fact well known to be. The music would reinforce rather than counterstate the melancholy tale of woe—negative emphasis being the point at issue—and the choreography most suitable for the Saturday Night Function would also be entirely appropriate for the traditional downhome Sunday Morning Service.

Which is not at all the same as saying that blues lyrics are unimportant. They may be mumbled, jumbled, or even scat-riffed, but they play a definitive role in the fundamental ritual of purification, affirmation, and celebration nonetheless. Also, in as much as the purpose of the incantation, percussion, and dance ritual of which the lyrics are a part involves ridding the atmosphere of demons, it is only natural that some will emphasize and in effect document misery. But that is only to say that blues lyrics often address themselves to the blues as such. It is not to say that blues music is not blues music without such lyrics. If such were the case, *The St. Louis Blues*, which has melancholy words, would qualify, but, to the consternation of most working blues musicians, such universally accepted classics as *The Memphis Blues* and *Beale Street Blues*, the words of which celebrate good times and good-time places, would not.

But with or without words, so far as working blues musicians are concerned, *The Memphis Blues* and *Beale Street Blues* are performed in slow and medium tempos, while *The St. Louis Blues* may be played in any tempo, and perhaps as often as not is taken medium- to up-tempo to hot. There is Bessie Smith's slow-drag version, for example, recorded in 1925, which is performed as a conventional, albeit idiomatic, lament in which the mournful voice detailing the plight of the victim is reinforced by a tearful harmonium and is perhaps just barely counterstated by the playful elegance of Louis Armstrong's cornet obbligato. But there is also Armstrong's own bookity-bookity up-tempo solo plus riff-chorus-response instrumental version (RCA Victor LJM 1005) recorded in 1933, that moves right through counterstatement to exuberant celebration, wiping out far more gloom in the process than is suggested by the lyrics in the first place. Then there is another

83

(Top, left) Earl Hines, also known as Fatha Hines, the innovator of the Armstrong-derived trumpetlike piano style. In 1928 he was pianist on a number of the finest recordings in the Armstrong canon, including *West End Blues, Weather Bird, Beau Koo Jack, Fireworks, Muggles, Basin Street Blues,* and *Hear Me Talkin' to Ya.* Between 1928 and 1948 he led one of the greatest orchestras of all time. (Bottom) Louis Armstrong pointing to singer Velma Middleton doing a novelty act with guitarist Lawrence Lucie.

Louis Armstrong the artist as Man the Player: "Look at them cats gittin' away. Look like they after me here. Looka here! But I'm ready, I'm ready. So help me, I'm ready. . . ."

Armstrong version, a medium-tempo vocal recorded in the 1950s (Phillips B07038L), with Velma Middleton singing the standard lyrics fairly straight and Armstrong substituting a new set of his own, which shifts the subject from lost love to insouciant sexuality.

There is also, among other festive treatments too numerous to list, Earl Hines's boogie-woogie arrangement for piano and orchestra, which became a big popular hit in the 1940s. But then long before the heyday of boogie woogie—which, it so happens, is by functional definition blues music played eight to the bar in medium- or up-tempo over a steady bass or left hand—instrumentalists were ragging and jazzing blues choruses. W. C. Handy's band musicians are said to have begun jazzing the breaks on *The Memphis Blues* (erstwhile *Mister Crump*) on the very first performance, and there is good reason to believe that such jazzing was already a part of the stock in trade of the folk musicians whose work Handy used as his point of departure. It was by all accounts already the forte of the legendary Buddy Bolden before the turn of the century. By the way, *Bolden's Blues*, which others called *Buddy Bolden's Blues* has been dated as of 1902, some seven years before Handy's *Mister Crump*, of 1909, which he redid and renamed *The Memphis Blues* in 1912. And Jelly Roll Morton, whose orchestrated extensions, elaborations, and refinements of blues music represent achievements of far greater significance than Handy's tunes, seems to have been ragging, stomping, jazzing, and riffing everything within earshot at least as early as 1900.

In point of fact, up-tempo treatment alone is of itself enough to contradict, repudiate and transcend lyrics far more downhearted than those of *The St. Louis Blues*. But as is also entirely consistent with the festive and affirmative nature of the traditional Saturday Night Function, and the vaudeville show too, for that matter, when *The Memphis Blues* and *Beale Street Blues* are rendered in medium or slow-drag tempo, the effect is not to negate or even diminish but rather to reiterate the goodtime-oriented message of the lyrics. Far from being incompatible with an atmosphere of enjoyment, the slow-drag tempo is, as the very notion of the fabled Easy Rider implies, a key factor operating to create that idiomatic groove of down-to-earth, person-to-person intimacy that is as inimical to gloom and doom as is the up-tempo stomp, the jump, or the shout.

86

Still the notion that all blues lyrics are necessarily mournful has become so deeply embedded over the years that any reference to *singing* the blues is likely to suggest the act of crying over misfortune, or moaning and groaning in misery and wretchedness, whining for sympathy over one's mean lot in life, voicing a complaint, or just plain bellyaching—infinitely more instantaneously than it ever evokes the simple concrete image of a musical performance, even of melancholy lyrics! On the other hand, when working musicians speak of playing the blues their terminology is not only consistent with what actually happens in a musical performance, but is no less applicable to the vocalist than to instrumentalists.

Blues musicians play music not only in the theatrical sense that actors play or stage a performance, but also in the general sense of playing for recreation, as when participating in games of skill. They also play in the sense of gamboling, in the sense that is to say, of fooling around or kidding around with, toying with, or otherwise having fun with. Sometimes they also improvise and in the process they elaborate, extend, and refine. But what they do in all instances involves the technical skill, imagination, talent, and eventually the taste that adds up to artifice. And of course such is the overall nature of play, which is so often a form of reenactment to begin with, that sometimes it also amounts to ritual.

By the same token, to the extent that references to singing the blues have come to suggest crying over misfortune, there is also likely to be the implication that blues music does not require artifice but is rather a species of direct emotional expression in the raw, the natural outpouring of personal anxiety and anguish, which in addition to reinforcing the old confusion of blues music with a case of blues as such, also ignores what a blues performance so obviously is. It is precisely an artful contrivance, designed for entertainment and aesthetic gratification; and its effectiveness depends on the mastery by one means or another of the fundamentals of the craft of music in general and a special sensitivity to the nuances of the idiom in particular.

When working musicians (whether they execute by ear or by score) announce that they are about to play the blues, what they most often mean is either that the next number on the program is composed in the traditional twelve-bar blues-chorus form, or that they are about to use the traditional twelve-bar chorus or stanza as

87

Billie Holiday, 1915–59, also known as Lady Day, was one of the great vocal stylists. She sang with the orchestras of Count Basie and Artie Shaw and recorded with Benny Goodman and Paul Whiteman, among others, but attained her great prominence as a solo attraction. Sensational publicity about her personal problems was such that for many people her singing came to represent the pathetic sound of an attractive but wretched woman crying in self-pity. And perhaps some of the torch-type pop songs in her repertoire seem to suggest the same thing. But the great and lasting distinction of Billie Holiday is not based on her highly publicized addiction to narcotics (a show-biz rather than a

blues-idiom phenomenon) but on her deliberate use of her voice as an Armstrong-derived instrumental extension. Not that she was ever given to scat-singing. On the contrary, she almost always delivered her lyrics not only with verbal precision but with conviction. Nevertheless, time and again she used to say she didn't think of herself as singing but as blowing a horn; and at her best she achieved an emotional impact akin to Bessie Smith's, an elegant inventiveness suggestive of Armstrong's trumpet (and voice) plus that special intensity that Lester Young could generate with cool understatement.

★
DECCA
PERSONALITY SERIES
REG. U.S. PAT. OFF.
MARCA REGISTRADA
MANUFACTURED BY DECCA RECORDS, INC., NEW YORK, U.S.A.

(73300)   Vocal
                                    with Orchestra

GOOD MORNING HEARTACHE
(Irene Higginbotham-Ervin Drake-Dan Fisher)

BILLIE HOLIDAY

23676 A

the basis for improvisation. They do not mean that they are about to display their own raw emotions. They are not really going to be crying, grieving, groaning, moaning, or shouting and screaming. They mean that they are about to proceed in terms of a very specific technology of stylization.

Playing
the Blues

Sometimes it all begins with the piano player vamping till ready, a vamp being an improvised introduction consisting of anything from the repetition of a chordal progression as a warm-up exercise to an improvised overture. Sometimes the vamp has already begun even before the name of the next number is given. Some singers, for instance, especially those who provide their own accompaniment on piano or guitar, use it as much as background for a running line of chatter, commentary, or mock didacticism as to set the mood and tempo for the next selection. Also, sometimes it is used to maintain the ambiance of the occasion and sometimes to change it.

Then the composition as such, which is made up of verses (optional), choruses (refrains), riffs, and breaks, begins. Some blues compositions such as Handy's *Yellow Dog Blues* have an introductory or verse section which establishes the basis for the choral refrain. Many, like Bessie Smith's *Long Old Road* and Big Joe Turner's *Piney Brown's Blues*, do not, and in practice perhaps more often than not the verse is omitted by singers as well as instrumentalists. But whether there is a vamp and/or a verse section, the main body of a blues composition consists of a series of choruses derived from the traditional three-line-stanza form. There may be as many choruses as the musician is inspired to play, unless there are such predetermined restrictions as recording space, broadcast time, or duration of a standard popular dance tune.

The traditional twelve-bar blues stanza-chorus consists of three lines of four bars each. But there are four bars of music in each line and only two bars (plus one beat) of lyric space:

	1ST BAR	2ND BAR
WORDS	Going to Chicago	Sorry but I can't take you
MUSIC	1 - 2 - 3 - 4	1 - 2 - 3 - 4 - 1
	3rd Bar	4th Bar
MUSIC	2 - 3 - 4	1 - 2 - 3 - 4
	5th Bar	6th Bar
WORDS	Going to Chicago	Sorry but I can't take you
MUSIC	1 - 2 - 3 - 4	1 - 2 - 3 - 4 - 1
	7th Bar	8th Bar
MUSIC	2 - 3 - 4	1 - 2 - 3 - 4
	9th Bar	10th Bar
WORDS	S'Nothing in Chicago	That a monkey woman can do
MUSIC	1 - 2 - 3 - 4	1 - 2 - 3 - 4 - 1
	11th Bar	12th Bar
MUSIC	2 - 3 - 4	1 - 2 - 3 - 4

Which by the way also means that there is always approximately twice as much music in a blues chorus as lyric space—even when it is a vocal chorus and the singer is performing a cappella and has to hum and/or drum his own fills.

Some choruses are refrain stanzas played by an instrumental ensemble, apparently a derivation and extension of the vocal choir. Some are played by a single instrument representing a choir. Originally a chorus, which is derived from the same root as *choreography*, was a dance and by extension a group of dancers (as it still is in musical comedies) and by further extension it also became an ensemble or a band of musicians who played for dancers. In ancient Greek drama it was the group of dancers and chanters who provided the necessary background, so to speak, for the solo performer or protagonist. Hence eventually the passages of the European oratorio which are performed by the choir, whether in unison or in polyphony, as opposed to the solo passages.

In most conventional compositions the chorus or refrain is the part that is repeated by all available voices or instruments. But sometimes musicians refer to the solos as choruses. Duke Ellington, for example, used to announce that the first chorus of his theme song would be played by the pianist (himself); then he would sit down and improvise an extended solo of any number of

W. C. Handy, 1873–1958, whose long career as an all-purpose professional musician included employment as itinerant quartet and glee-club singer, music teacher, bandmaster for Mahara Minstrels, conductor of outdoor bandstand concerts of "classical" music, leader of parade and dance bands, songwriter, and publisher, is remembered mainly as the composer of *The St. Louis Blues, The Memphis Blues, Yellow Dog Blues, Beale Street Blues, Aunt Hagar's Children, Ole Miss, Loveless Love,* and *Chantez les Bas.*

stanzas. Likewise the singer's solo of a blues arrangement may consist of one or several choruses but is also known as the vocal chorus.

Blues musicians also make extensive use of riff choruses. A blues riff is a brief musical phrase that is repeated, sometimes with very subtle variations, over the length of a stanza as the chordal pattern follows its normal progression. Sometimes the riff chorus is used as background for the lead melody and as choral *response* to the solo *call* line. But many arrangements are structured largely and sometimes almost entirely of riff choruses. In Count Basie's original recording of *One o'Clock Jump* (Decca DXSB-7170) for example, the piano begins with a brief traditional music-hall or vaudeville vamp and a solo and is followed by a tenor-sax solo backed by a trumpet-ensemble riff. Then comes a trombone solo over a reed-ensemble riff; and a second tenor saxophone is backed by the trumpet ensemble playing a different riff; and a trumpet solo is backed by another reed-ensemble riff. Then there is a twelve-bar rhythm chorus punctuated by solo piano riffs; and finally there is a sequence of three more ensemble riff choruses (the trumpets and trombones repeating a call-and-response figure over and over while the reeds play three different unison riffs) as a climax or outchorus.

When they are effective, riffs always seem as spontaneous as if they were improvised in the heat of performance. So much so that riffing is sometimes regarded as being synonymous with improvisation. But such is not always the case by any means. Not only are riffs as much a part of some arrangements and orchestrations as the lead melody, but many consist of nothing more than stock phrases, quotations from some familiar melody, or even clichés that just happen to be popular at the moment. But then in the jam session, which seems to have been the direct source of the Kansas City riff style as featured by Bennie Moten, Count Basie, and Andy Kirk, among others, improvisation includes spontaneous appropriation (or inspired allusion, which sometimes is also a form of signifying) no less than on-the-spot invention. Moreover, as is also the case with the best of the so-called unaltered found objects on exhibition in some of the better avant-garde art galleries, the invention of creative process lies not in the originality of the phrase as such, but in the way it is used in a frame of reference!

Duke Ellington (top, left) and Count Basie (top, right) masters of the piano vamp for full orchestra and past masters also of the art of comping (backing soloists with imaginative accompanimental chordal punctuations) on the piano and also with sections and with the total ensemble. In actual performance jump music, as in *One o'Clock Jump,* is indistinguishable from a stomp, as in *Panassié Stomp,* or swing, as in *Moten Swing.* The dance steps are different, of course, but even so one can jump to a stomp and swing; stomp to a jump and swing; or swing to a jump and a stomp.

Background or accompanimental riffs not only provide a harmonic setting for the solo melody, but sometimes they also function as the ensemble response to the solo call, much the same as
the Amen Corner moans and the chants of the generalcongrega-
tion reply to the solo voice of the minister (and the prayer leader)
during the Sunday Morning Service. Which is also to say that they
may sometimes serve as an exhortation to the soloist. But sometimes what with all the shouting and stomping, it is also somewhat
as if the ensembles were either chasing or fleeing, or otherwise
contesting the soloist. At other times it is not so much like a contest
as like a game of leapfrog.

Nothing is likely to seem more spontaneous than call-and-
response passages, especially in live performances, where they
almost always seem to grow directly out of the excitement of the
moment, as if the musicians were possessed by some secular equivalent of the Holy Ghost. But as is no less the practice in the
Sunday Morning Service, the responses are not only stylized (and
stylized in terms of a specific idiom, to boot), but are almost always
led by those who have a special competence in such devices. After
all, no matter how deeply moved a musician may be, whether by
personal, social, or even aesthetic circumstances, he must always
play notes that fulfill the requirements of the context, a feat which
presupposes far more skill and taste than raw emotion.

Obviously, such skill and taste are matters of background, experience, and idiomatic orientation. What they represent is not
natural impulse but the refinement of habit, custom, and tradition
become second nature, so to speak. Indeed on close inspection
what was assumed to have been unpremeditated art is likely to be
largely a matter of conditioned reflex, which is nothing other than
the end product of discipline, or in a word, training. In any case
practice is as indispensable to blues musicians as to any other kind.
As a very great trumpet player, whose soulfulness was never in
question, used to say, "Man, if you ain't got the chops for the dots,
ain't nothing happening."

That musicians whose sense of incantation and percussion was
conditioned by the blues idiom in the first place are likely to
handle its peculiarities with greater ease and assurance than outsiders of comparable or even superior conventional skill should
surprise no one. But that does not mean, as is so often implied, if

not stated outright, that their expression is less a matter of artifice, but rather that they have had more practice with the technical peculiarities involved and have also in the normal course of things acquired what is tantamount to a more refined sensitivity to the inherent nuances.

All of which makes what is only a performance seem like a direct display of natural reflexes, because it obscures the technical effort. But blues performances are based on a mastery of a very specific technology of stylization by one means or another nonetheless. And besides, effective make-believe is the whole point of all the aesthetic technique and all the rehearsals from the outset. Nor does the authenticity of any performance of blues music depend upon the musician being true to his own private feelings. It depends upon his idiomatic ease and consistency.

●

Another technical device peculiar to blues music is the break, which is a very special kind of ad-lib bridge passage or cadenzalike interlude between two musical phrases that are separated by an interruption or interval in the established cadence. Customarily there may be a sharp shotlike accent and the normal or established flow of the rhythm and the melody stop, much the same as a sentence seems to halt, but only pauses at a colon. Then the gap, usually of not more than four bars, is filled in most often but not always by a solo instrument, whose statement is usually impromptu or improvised even when it is a quotation or a variation from some well-known melody. Then when the regular rhythm is picked up again (while the ensemble, if any, falls back in), it is as if you had been holding your breath.

Louis Armstrong's Hot Seven recording of *Weary Blues* (Columbia Golden Era Series CL 852)—which, by the way, expresses not weariness but a stomping exuberance—contains a number of easily identified breaks. The first follows the opening waillike ensemble chant and is filled by a clarinet. The second follows the first full chorus by the ensemble and is also filled in by the clarinet. The third, fourth, and fifth are filled in by the banjo. The sixth, seventh, and eighth are filled by the tuba; and the ninth by Armstrong himself on trumpet.

In a sense Armstrong's second solo in *Potato Head Blues* (Columbia Golden Era Series CL 852) represents a more elaborate

99

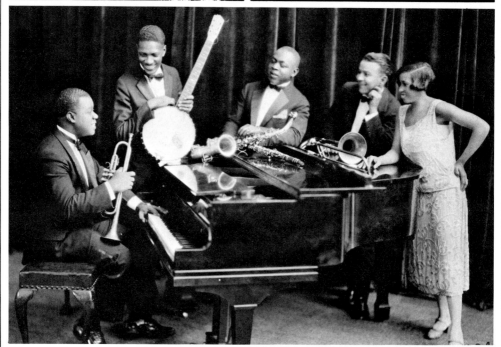

(Bottom) Louis Armstrong's Hot Five, (left to right) Armstrong, trumpet; Johnny St. Cyr, banjo; Johnny Dodds, clarinet; Kid Ory, trombone; and Lil Hardin, piano, existed only as a recording unit. Contrary to the label, however, there were seven musicians on *Weary Blues* (Chicago, May 11, 1927) as on *Willie the Weeper* (Chicago, May 7, 1927): Armstrong, St. Cyr, Johnny Dodds, Lil Hardin, with John Thomas substituting for Kid Ory, plus Peter Briggs on tuba and Baby Dodds the drummer, who is heard on cymbals.

At the time of this publicity shot, circa 1930, Louis
Armstrong had gone beyond such mentors as Bunk
Johnson and King Oliver (and such great rivals as
Freddy Keppard, as well) and had not only established
his supremacy on his instrument but had also become
the crucial stylistic influence on the idiom at large.
Armstrong's mastery of the cornet and trumpet consisted of unsurpassed beauty of tone, an impeccable
sense of beat and phrasing, an unerring sense of elegance, plus an incredible ability to invent fresh and perfectly constructed patterns against almost any background. His solos were so free of clichés that few have
become dated over the years.

use of the options of the break. It consists of sixteen consecutive two-bar phrases, each filling a break following a heavy beat that functions as the musical equivalent of a colon. Then there is also Duke Ellington's *C-Jam Blues* (RCA Victor LPV 541) in which each of the five solo choruses, beginning with Ray Nance on violin, starts out as a two-bar-break improvisation. Ellington's title *Bugle Breaks* (Jazz Society AA 502) is quite simply a literal reference to the structure of what is one of his versions of *Bugle Call Rag*, which he plays as if mainly to feature four trumpet break-fills plus one by trombone and two by a trumpet ensemble.

Break passages are far more likely to be improvised on the spot than riff figures. But sometimes improvising on the break is also referred to as riffing, as Armstrong does on his recording of *Lazy River* (Columbia Golden Era Series C 854) when he finishes scatting a break and chuckles (not unlike a painter stepping back to admire his own brush stroke): "Boy, if I ain't riffing this evening I hope something."

Many riffs no doubt begin as just such on-the-spot break-fill improvisations as the one Armstrong was so pleased with. Because, as evolution of the so-called head or unwritten arrangement/composition suggests, as soon as the special ones are played they are almost always made a part of a score (written or not) either by the player or somebody else.

Sometimes the riffs replace the original melody, or indeed become the melodic line of an extension that may be a new composition. Duke Ellington's *Crescendo in Blue* and *Diminuendo in Blue* sound like such an extension of *The St. Louis Blues*, and when his arrangement for a vocal version of *The St. Louis Blues* (RCA Victor LPM 306) is heard with the singer out of the range of the microphone as in the recording (Pima 01 and 02) made during a performance at the Chicago Civic Opera, November 11, 1946, then it sounds like still another composition. Similarly, the only scrap of the melody of the original *St. Louis Blues* in the version arranged for Dizzy Gillespie by Budd Johnson (RCA Victor LJM 1009) is Gillespie's trumpet-solo approximation of the vocal lines: "St. Louis woman with her diamond rings/pulls that man around by her apron strings." The rest is mostly riff choruses plus a saxophone solo plus the trumpet playing what amounts to a sort of mini-concerto which, by the way, includes a bop-style break daz-

Dizzy Gillespie (top, left) wearing beret and horn-rim glasses, fad symbols of bop in the 1940s; (top, right) performing; and (bottom) on the bandstand with Tommy Potter, bass; Charlie Parker, alto; and John Coltrane, tenor. Gillespie, an irrepressible showman and prankster, belongs in the triumvirate of definitive trumpet style setters with Armstrong and Miles Davis. In the process of establishing bop as the avant-garde movement of the mid-forties he also became one of the most important bandleaders of his time.

zlingly executed by Gillespie—the likes of which was matched only by Charlie Parker.

What with recordings making them available for the most careful study through endless repetition, break passages are also memorized, repeated, imitated, and incorporated into scores. It is not at all unusual for one musician's break to become another's riff chorus—or lead melody. The break with which King Oliver opens his cornet solo in *Snag It* (Decca Jazz Heritage Series DL 79246) seems to have been considered as being in the public domain as soon as other musicians heard it, and has been used as a Buddy Bolden-like clarion call to revelry ever since, not only by other soloists but by arrangers as well. Blues musicians across the nation spent long hours rehearsing and appropriating Armstrong's breaks on *Beau Koo Jack* (Okeh 8680) to name only one, and the same thing happened with Charlie Parker's alto break on *Night in Tunisia* (Baronet Records B 105).

In other words, when Armstrong said what he said on *Lazy River*, he knew very well whereof he spoke. A riff is a musical phrase used as a refrain chorus, background chorus, response chorus, echo chorus, and so on; and a riff tune is one constructed mainly of riff choruses; but the process of riffing (from the verb, *to riff*) refers not only to making riff phrases and playing riff choruses and substituting riffs for melodies as written, but also to improvisation in general. Thus the term *riff session* often refers to a jam session.

•

Among other fundamental prerequisites for playing (and playing with) blues music are such essentials of rhythmic nuance as beat and syncopation. Keeping the beat or beating time, whether by foot tapping, hand clapping, finger snapping, head rocking, or by means of the bass drum, bass fiddle, tuba, piano pedal, and so on, may seem ever so natural to the uninitiated listener, but it is a matter of very precise musicianship nevertheless. The more precise the musicianship, which is to say, the musical know-how, discipline, and skill, the more natural-seeming the beat—as natural in effect as the human pulse. One of the most precise, distinctive, and highly celebrated rhythm sections in the entire history of blues music was the so-called All American Rhythm Section (Jo Jones, drums; Walter Page, bass; Freddie Greene, guitar; and Count Basie, piano) of the Count Basie Orchestra from the mid-

King Oliver, 1885–1938, six years younger than Bunk Johnson and four years older than Freddy Keppard, began his apprenticeship in New Orleans during the high times of Buddy Bolden, and by the time he left for Chicago in 1917 had become the cornet player and bandleader in Storyville (then closed by the U.S. Navy). In Chicago, Oliver, the most direct and decisive influence on Louis Armstrong, established himself as the first great New Orleans bandleader of national prominence. Along with Jelly Roll Morton, Armstrong, and Ellington, King Oliver was a seminal influence on the Kansas City musicians under whom Charlie Parker served his apprenticeship.

1930s to the late 1940s. And yet the drummer not only seemed to be the most nonchalant person on hand, it was also almost always as if you felt the beat more than you actually heard it, which of course was exactly the way it should be. Sometimes, indeed it was as if Jo Jones only whispered the beat.

At the same time nonchalance was also the ultimate effect created by the flamboyant showmanship of Chick Webb. All of the stamping and sweating of Gene Krupa, a Webb-derived white drummer of the so-called Swing Era, gave the impression that he was putting himself so totally into the act of beating it out that he was possessed (for the time being) by some violent tom-tom-oriented savage force. But with Webb it was as if the breathtaking rolls lightninglike breaks and juggler-type stick twirling were designed for the express purpose of making it appear that the drummer was not at all preoccupied with such an elementary matter as timekeeping—or that keeping musical time was so natural that he was ever so free to fool around while doing so.

Yet keeping the appropriate beat is hardly more natural to U.S. Negro musicians than it was for their drum-oriented forebears in ancestral Africa, where musicians were always required to be thoroughly trained and formally certified professionals. To the Africans from whom the dance-beat disposition of U.S. Negroes is derived, rhythm was far more a matter of discipline than of the direct expression of personal feelings. African drummers had to serve a long period of rigidly supervised apprenticeship before being entrusted with such an awesome responsibility as carrying the beat!

Nor is the process of beat, off-beat, or weak-beat accentuation known as syncopation any less a matter of competent musicianship. Used as required by the blues idiom, syncopation seems as natural as the contractions, liaisons, slurs, ellipses, and accents of a normal speaking manner. But the fact that syncopation is necessarily idiomatic means that it is a customary or stylized rather than a natural aspect of expression. Thus it can be refined, elaborated, extended, abstracted, and otherwise played with. It is, as the juxtaposition of any blues recording with any piece of conventional European music will bear out at once, something that blues musicians play with in the sense of making use of it as an indispensable device, as well as in the sense of having fun.

106

(Top, left) Chick Webb, one of the greatest and most widely imitated of all dance-band drummers, led the orchestra that became synonymous with stomping at the Savoy, the most famous ballroom in Harlem during the so-called Swing Era. (Top, right) African drums were the ancestral source of the dance-beat emphasis of blues music. (Bottom) The Count Basie rhythm section in a recording studio, 1938.

Beat and syncopation are also a matter of taste. But what is taste if not a matter of idiomatic preference? As in the kitchen, taste is a sense of recipe, a sense of the most flavorful proportion of the ingredients. In music it is a sense of nuance that defies notation in the same way as, say, a very fine downhome cook's offhand-seeming use of a pinch of this, a touch of that, and a smidgen of the other, confounds the follower of precisely measured formulas. In both instances the proportions are matters of idiomatic orientation. Thus the preference is also a matter of conditioning which is a result of the most careful training however informal. Indeed, in such cases the more subtle the training, the more likely the outcome to seem like second nature.

Still another fundamental aspect of blues musicianship that is often mistaken as a natural phenomenon is tonal coloration. But once again the quality of voice that notes are given in the actual performance of blues music is, uniquely personal endowments aside, perhaps mainly a matter of idiomatic orientation. Which is to say that it is perhaps mostly a matter of tonal stylization derived from other performers. Before Bessie Smith there was Ma Rainey. Before Louis Armstrong there were King Oliver and Bunk Johnson. Before Duke Ellington there were Jelly Roll Morton, King Oliver, and Armstrong, as well as the Harlem Stride piano players and the Fletcher Henderson orchestra.

That timbre and vibrato are devices that Bessie Smith and Louis Armstrong played with much the same as they played with beat should be so obvious that it need be mentioned only in passing, and no less obscure is the profound influence of Bessie Smith and Louis Armstrong on the tonal coloration of other musicians over the years. But perhaps the most clearcut indication of the blues musician's involvement with tonal coloration is some of the accessory equipment such as wa-wa and Harmon mutes, plungers, and aluminum, felt, and cardboard derbies for brass; an assortment of sticks, brushes, mallets, and various other gadgets for voicing drums; and so on. Duke Ellington's use of timbre and vibrato as orchestral devices, as well as other extensions and refinements, made him the preeminent composer/conductor of blues music.

The tonal nuances of blues music are also a matter of singers playing with their voices as if performing on an instrument, and of

108

(Top, left) Jelly Roll Morton, 1885–1941, among whose compositions are such classics of the idiom as *Buddy Bolden's Blues, Dead Man Blues, Original Jelly Roll Blues, Winin' Boy Blues, King Porter Stomp, Kansas City Stomp, Grandpa's Spells, Wolverine Blues,* and *The Pearls,* was the great forerunner of the blues-idiom arranger-composer-conductor-performer. (Top, right) Willie "The Lion" Smith, 1897–1970, was one of the greatest of the Harlem Stride piano players, whose style (along with that of James P. Johnson) was an important influence on Duke Ellington. (Bottom, left) Bunk Johnson, 1879–1949, was an important link between Louis Armstrong and Buddy Bolden. (Bottom, right) Ma Rainey, 1886–1939, the first professional blues singer to gain national recognition.

Fletcher Henderson, 1898–1952, was at one time pianist and arranger for such headline blues mamas as young Ethel Waters and Bessie Smith. He is of far greater historical significance, however, as leader of the first big dance orchestra to perform primarily in terms of scores constructed on the dynamics of blues-idiom statement, including improvised solos and riff extensions. The Henderson orchestra was the model for most of the so-called big swing bands, including those of Duke Ellington and Count Basie. Indeed it was to Henderson that the first Basie band turned for written scores to augment its repertoire (consisting mostly of heads) as it moved from the Kansas City area into the national spotlight.

(Top) Fletcher Henderson and orchestra circa 1924, during the epoch-making sojourn of Louis Armstrong. (Left to right) Howard Scott, trumpet; Coleman Hawkins, tenor sax; Armstrong; Charlie Dixon, banjo; Henderson, piano; Kaiser Marshall, drums; Buster Bailey, clarinet; Elmer Chambers, trumpet; Charlie Green, trombone; Bob Escudero, tuba; and Don Redman, alto sax and arrangements. (Bottom) Fletcher Henderson and Orchestra, 1936. (Left to right) Chu Berry, tenor sax; Joe Thomas, trumpet; Horace Henderson, piano, arranger; Sid Catlett, drums; Fletcher Henderson, piano, arranger; Dick Vance, trumpet; Teddy Lewis, vocalist; Buster Bailey, clarinet, alto sax; Elmer Williams, tenor sax; Ed Cuffee, trombone; Roy Eldridge, trumpet; Israel Crosby, bass; Fernando Arbello, trombone; Bob Lessey, guitar; Jerome Don Pasquall, alto sax.

(Top) Ellington Brass, 1932. (Left to right) Freddy Jenkins, trumpet; Lawrence Brown, trombone; Cootie Williams, trumpet; Juan Tizol, trombone. (Not in picture: Arthur Whetsol, trumpet; and Tricky Sam Nanton, trombone.) (Bottom) Ellington Woodwinds. Johnny Hodges, alto; Otto Hardwick, alto; Barney Bigard, clarinet and tenor; Harry Carney, baritone, clarinet, bass clarinet, and alto. Ellington did not feature the tenor sax as an important solo voice until Ben Webster became a regular in 1939.

Louis Armstrong, whose singing style has been as definitive an influence as his trumpet style, was using his voice as an instrument long before he extemporized his first recorded scat vocal during a mishap in the studio while making *Heebie Jeebies*.

instrumentalists using their brasses, woodwinds, strings, keyboards, and percussion as extensions of the human voice. Perhaps reciprocal "voicing" is inherent in the old call-and-response or voice-and-echo pattern as produced by the ratio of instrumental accompaniment space to the lyric space in the basic traditional blues stanza. But, inherent or not, the so-called scat vocal with which the singer plays instrumental music with his voice by using nonsense syllables instead of the words of a lyric is only the most patent form of vocal instrumentation. When Louis Armstrong began singing, it was very much as if he were using his voice to supplement what he had been saying with his trumpet all along—some of which was backtalk for Ma Rainey (as on *Countin' the Blues* [Milestone M 4721] for example) and Bessie Smith (as on *Reckless Blues* and *Sobbing Hearted Blues* [Columbia G 30818]). Nor was the voice of any scat singer ever played more like an instrument than that of Bessie Smith, who, as has been pointed out, could get the same musical effect with the most banal, inconsequential, and indeed *non sequitur* lyrics as with those of the highest poetic quality, which she often misquoted.

On the other hand such was the vocal orientation of Duke Ellington's genius that in addition to achieving the most highly distinctive overall instrumental orchestral sound (made up of instrumental voice extensions), he not only played his orchestra as if it were a single instrument (to an extent that cannot be claimed for any other composer or conductor) but expressed himself on it as if the three-man rhythm section, three trombones, four to six trumpets, five woodwinds (plus occasional strings) were actually the dimensions of one miraculously endowed human voice. As in the tearful hoarseness of the shouting brass ensemble in the call-and-response outchorus of *Perdido* (RCA Victor LPM 1364) for instance; the somewhat worn-out and breathless ensemble woodwinds calling or answering the flippant piano after the drum roll following the stratospheric trumpet solo in *Let the Zoomers Drool* (Fairmont FA 1007); as in the querulous mumbling mixed in with all the stridency of the first trumpet solo of *Hollywood Hangover* (Saga 6926), as in the Armstrong-like gravel tone of the main theme ensemble passages of *Blue Ramble* (Columbia C 31 27).

Such is also the nature of the craft involved in the fusion of incantation and percussion known as blues music that even as they

Duke Ellington, arranger, composer, conductor, piano player, and urbane matinee idol, as he looked during the late 1920s. Blues orchestrations are often based on existing twelve-bar blues ballads and thirty-two-bar pop tunes just as many of the plays in ancient Greece and Elizabethan England, the commedia dell'arte presentations during the Italian Renaissance, and the skits of the old American minstrels and medicine shows were based on existing story lines.

115

play as if on extensions of human voices, blues musicians proceed at the very same time as if their strings, keyboards, brasses, and woodwinds were also extensions of talking drums, fulfilling the conventional timekeeping function while the designated rhythm section, in addition to filling its traditional role, also functions as an instrumental extension of the human voice, making vocal-type statements along with other instrumental voices.

Of course the conventional tonalities inherent in the very nature of keyboards, strings, brasses, and woodwinds are also utilized as such in the process, just as in the most representational painting where paint is used as paint, brush strokes as brush strokes, while the canvas remains a canvas. Inevitably the idiomatic extensions are based squarely on the fact, or at any rate the supposition, that musicians can do certain things on instruments that cannot be done with the human voice—or with talking drums (which seem to have been used for the same reason in the first place). Nor is there likely to be much doubt that such reedmen, say, as Sidney Bechet, Coleman Hawkins, Lester Young, Johnny Hodges, Charlie Parker, and Harry Carney preferred playing saxophone to being singers—or drummers.

Nevertheless, one way for those whose ears are uninitiated to the idiom to become oriented to blues music is for them to begin by listening as if each blues composition was being played by so many talking drums, some voiced as guitars and banjos, some as pianos, trumpets, trombones, saxophones, clarinets, and so on.

Sometimes, as in *Diminuendo in Blue* and *Crescendo in Blue*, not only do the trumpets and trombones extend the shouting and hey-saying voice of the downhome church choir, but they also take the lead in doing drum work and drum talk at the same time. Nor for the most part are the terms in which any of the brasses or woodwinds speak on Count Basie's *Swinging the Blues, Time Out,* and *Panassié Stomp* (Decca DXSB 7170). And what a master drummer among drummers Louis Armstrong becomes with his trumpet and with his voice as well on *Swing that Music* (Decca Jazz Heritage Series DL 79225).

Drum talk is not only what the accompanying guitar, banjo, or piano answers or echoes the folk blues with, and not only what such singers answer and echo themselves with when they hum, beat out or otherwise furnish their own comps, fills, and frills; but

116

(Top, left) Leadbelly, 1888-1949, with his notorious twelve-string train-whistle guitar. (Top, right) Washboard Sam and his long-gone locomotive washboard. (Bottom) Cannon's Jug Stompers, well-known orchestrators of locomotive onomatopoeia, circa 1930. (Left to right) Gus Cannon, jug and banjo; John Estes, guitar; Noah Lewis, harmonica. Many guitar players also doubled on harmonica.

117

it is also most likely to be what all blues singers do even as they play with their voices as if on brasses, keyboards, strings, and woodwinds. But then the use of the break as a fundamental element of blues musicianship already provides an unmistakable clue to how closely blues-idiom statement is geared to the syntax of the drummer. In any case it is a mistake for the uninitiated listener to approach blues music with the assumption that rhythm is only incidental to melody, as it tends to be in European music.

It is not enough, however, to say that blues musicians often play on their horns, their keyboards, and strings as if on drums. Nor is it enough to say that the drums are more African than European in that they keep rhythm and talk at the same time. The rhythmic emphasis of blues music is more obviously African than either the so-called blue note or the call-and-response pattern, but all the same, the actual voices of which all blues instrumentation is an extension speak primarily and definitively as well in the idiomatic accents and tonalities of U.S. Negroes down South. And what is more, not only do they speak about downhome experience, which is to say human experience as perceived by downhome people, but they speak also in the terms, including the onomatopoeia, of downhome phenomena.

So much so that what may once have been West African drum talk has in effect at any rate long since become the locomotive talk of the old steam-driven railroad trains as heard by downhome blackfolk on farms, in work camps, and on the outskirts of southern towns. Not that blues musicians in general are or ever were— or need be—as consciously involved with railroad onomatopoeia as the old-time harmonica players who were Leadbelly's forerunners seem so often to have been. But even so there is more than enough preoccupation with railroad imagery in blues titles, not to mention blues lyrics, to establish the no less mythological than pragmatic role of the old steam-driven locomotive as a fundamental element of immediate significance in the experience and hence the imagination of the so-called black southerners.

Also, as an actual phenomenon of crucial historical significance the old steam-driven railroad train with its heroic beat, its ceremonial bell, and heraldic as well as narrative whistle goes all the way back not only to the legendary times of John Henry and the steel-driving times that were the heyday of nationwide railroad con-

118

(Top) Downhome section gang with section boss (left) verifying alignment from a distance; ten section hands (center) rapping steel on steel; and section foreman:

> Hey, big boy cain't ya line em
> S'now big bo cain't ya line em
> Said big boy cain't ya line em
> *Bebap bap bebappity   bap bap bap*
> *Bebap bap bebappity   bap bap bap*
> *Bebap bap bebappity   bap bap bap*

(Bottom) Bluesteel percussion and vocal chorus plus soloist between renditions.

rails a-hummin'
train's a-comin'
got a mind to go

engine singin'
blue bell ringin'
hear that whistle blow

struction, but also to the ante-bellum period of the mostly metaphorical Underground Railroad that the Fugitive Slaves took from the House of Bondage to the Promised Land of Freedom.

The influence of the old smoke-chugging railroad-train engine on the sound of blues music may or may not have been as great as that of the downhome church, but both have been definitive, and sometimes it is hard to say which is the source of what. Item: As used in blues orchestrations one call-and-response sequence may have derived directly from the solo call of the minister and the ensemble response of the congregation in the church service; but another, say as in Louis Armstrong's recording of *Wolverine Blues* (Ace of Hearts AH 7), may well have come from the solo call of the train whistle and the ensemble response of the pumping pistons and rumbling boxcars; and there is a good chance that there are times when a little of both exists in each. Likewise, in church music, cymbals sound as Biblical as tambourines and timbrels, but what they are most likely to suggest when played by blues musicians is the keen percussive explosions of locomotive steam.

Similarly, some of the great variety of bell-like piano sounds that so many blues musicians, piano players in particular, like to play around with may sometimes be stylizations of church bells ringing for Sunday Morning Service, sending tidings, tolling for the dead, and so on; but most often they seem to be train bells. The bell-like piano chorus that Count Basie plays against the steady four/four of the bass fiddle, guitar, and cymbals in *One o'Clock Jump* is far more suggestive of the arrival and departure bell of a train pulling into or out of a station than of church bells of any kind.

And the same is essentially the case with train whistles. The influence of church music on blues music is sometimes very direct indeed. Not only do many blues musicians begin as church musicians, but, as is well known, many blues compositions are only secular adaptations of church tunes. Yet as much church-organ influence as may be heard in numberless blues-ensemble passages, the tonal coloration of most of Count Basie's ensemble passages (as on *9:20 Special* (Epic LN 1117) sounds much more like a sophisticated extension of the train-whistle stylizations that have long been the stock in trade of so many downhome harmonica players and guitar players than like church hymns, anthems, spirituals, and gospel music.

But then what with all the gospel trains and glory-bound specials and expresses and all the concern about passengers getting on board and on the right track in church music long before blues music as such came into existence, many of the stylizations of locomotive sounds may have come into the tonal vocabulary of blues musicians by way of the church in the first place rather than directly from the everyday world. Thus for one listener Duke Ellington's *Way Low* (Columbia Archives Series C 3L 39) begins with a church moan while for another it sounds like an orchestrated train whistle; both are at least consistent with the idiom.

Nor does the association in either case lead to the implication that blues music is primarily programmatic. It is not. Onomatopoeia is only a point of departure for the idiomatic play and interplay of what is essentially dance-beat-oriented percussion and incantation. Once voiced or played, even the most literal imitation of the sound of the most familiar everyday phenomenon becomes an element of musical stylization and convention. Thus the railroad sounds in such Ellington compositions as *Daybreak Express* (RCA Victor LVP 506), *Happy Go Lucky Local* (Allegro 1591 and Pima DC 01 and 02) and *The Old Circus Train Turn Around Blues* (Verve V40722) remain unmistakable. But even so, Ellington's unique nuances aside, what all the whistles, steam-driven pistons, bells, and echoes add up to is the long-since-traditional sound of blues-idiom dance-hall music. And, except in novelty numbers like Fletcher Henderson's *Alabamy Bound* (Columbia C 4L 19), musicians approach it not as a matter of railroad mimicry, but in terms of form and craft. Indeed, much goes to show that what musicians are always most likely to be mimicking (and sometimes extending and refining and sometimes counterstating) are the sounds of other musicians who have performed the same or similar compositions.

Thus for all the use Duke Ellington had already made of railroad onomatopoeia in his own compositions over the years, what his version of *9:20 Special* (Swing Treasury 105) mimics, elaborates, and extends is not the sound of an actual train but rather the melody, the KC 4/4 beat, the ensemble choruses and solos with which Earle Warren and the Count Basie Orchestra had already stylized the sound of what may have been the original *9:20*

125

Special—or may have been still another composition derived from other locomotive sounds that nobody now remembers as such. Anyway, what Ellington's own bell-ringing piano fingers play around with are the already abstract bell-like piano choruses of Count Basie, and the same holds for the ensemble passages. The train-whistle-like sonorities are still very much there for those who have ears for that sort of thing, indeed they may be even more obvious, especially in such woodwind passages as follow the first piano bridge. Nevertheless, the musicians are most likely to have approached the whole thing not as another version of a train, a somewhat slower train; but rather as an Ellington takeoff on a Basie jump number, to be played more like a mellow bounce than as an all-out hard-driving stomp.

●

Such is the stuff of which blues musicianship is made. It is not a matter of having the blues and giving direct personal release to the raw emotion brought on by suffering. It is a matter of mastering the elements of craft required by the idiom. It is a matter of idiomatic orientation and of the refinement of auditory sensibility in terms of idiomatic nuance. It is a far greater matter of convention, and hence tradition, than of impulse.

It is thus also far more a matter of imitation and variation and counterstatement than of originality. It is not so much what blues musicians bring out of themselves on the spur of the moment as what they do with existing conventions. Sometimes they follow them by extending that which they like or accept, and sometimes by counterstating that which they reject. Which is what W. C. Handy did to folk blues at a certain point. Which is what Bessie Smith seems to have done to Ma Rainey's singing style. It is clearly what Louis Armstrong did to what King Oliver and Bunk Johnson had already done to the trumpet style of Buddy Bolden himself. Count Basie extended the Harlem Stride extension of the ragtime piano in the very process of stripping it down for use as an element of Kansas City riff-style orchestration. The unchallenged supremacy of Duke Ellington is not based on pure invention but on the fact that his oeuvre represents the most comprehensive assimilation, counterstatement, and elaboration of most, if not all, of the elements of blues musicianship.

It was not so much what Charlie Parker did on impulse that

Ornithological references appear again and again in the titles of recordings by Charlie Parker, whose nickname was Bird as in Yardbird (his jive term for chicken). Parker's complete works include *Yardbird Suite, Blue Bird, Bird's Blues, Bird Feathers, Bird of Paradise, Chasin' the Bird, Carving the Bird, Bird Gets the Worm*, and *Ornithology*, an extension of *How High the Moon*, written for him by Benny Harris. But still and all, the chances are that no real-life bird ever actually flew like Charlie the Yardbird. As magnificent as the most beautiful birds look against the sky, they mostly only flap and glide—whereas Parker cut figures with the dance-beat elegance of the pilots of the old 332nd Fighter Group.

made him the formidable soloist and influential revolutionary stylist that he was, it was what he did in response to already existing procedures. His own widely quoted account of his evolution provides a concrete example of the dynamics of acceptance, rejection, and counterstatement, as it operates in the process of innovation:

> Now, I had been getting bored with the stereotyped changes that were being used all the time at that time, and I kept thinking there's bound to be something else. I could hear it sometimes, but I couldn't play it.
> Well, that night I was working over *Cherokee*, and as I did, I found that by using the higher intervals of a chord as a melody line and backing them with appropriately related changes, I could play the things I had been hearing.

Such is the nature of the blues-idiom tradition of stylization that what he played begins by being a most elegant extension of some of the innovations of Buster Smith and Lester Young heard in Kansas City back during the days of his apprenticeship.

As for the ritualistic significance of the essential playfulness involved in blues musicianship, it is in effect the very process of improvisation, elaboration, variation, extension, and refinement (or of just plain fooling around, for that matter) that makes sport of, and hence serves to put the blue demons of gloom and ultimate despair to flight. Much has been made of the personal anguish of Charlie Parker, perhaps even more than has been made of the tribulations of Bessie Smith, and indeed there is always some unmistakable evidence of the blues as such somewhere in all of his music, but they are always at bay somewhere in the background, never in the foreground, for there is probably no species of gloomy demon yet known to man that can tolerate the playful and sometimes insouciant and sometimes raucous elegance of the likes of Charlie Parker performing *Ko-Ko* (Savoy MG 12014), *Parker's Mood* (Savoy MG 12009), *Ornithology* and *Yardbird Suite* (Baronet Records B 105), or *Now is the Time* (Savoy MG 12001) or jamming on *Sweet Georgia Brown* (Milestone MSP 9035). And when the clip gets too fast for most dance couples, as it does on the famous break on *Night in Tunisia,* all they have to do is hold on to each other and listen as Parker makes the notes dance.

128

Swinging
the Blues

Once they started making phonograph records of it you could hear it almost any time of the day on almost any day of the week and almost anywhere that was far enough away from the church. Because not only did there seem to be at least one phonograph in almost every neighborhood from the very outset, but it was also as if that was the music that phonograph records were all about in the first place, which, incidentally, is also why the Victrola and the Gramophone, which were also called the graphonola and the talking machine, began by being condemned in so many Sunday Morning Sermons as the diabolical apparatus of the Devil's agents of wickedness.

Back before the first phonograph records there were the singing guitar strummers and pickers (and sometimes some harmonica blowers also) who used to play strolling (in half-time or deliberately out of time) along the street and while stashed on certain busy corners or sitting on certain store-front benches; and sometimes when not working in the honky-tonks until the wee hours of the morning like the piano players, they also used to play in certain yards and on certain porches in the summer twilight, and by certain firesides in the wintertime. And sometimes there also used to be one if not several on that part of the picnic grounds and in that part of the baseball field where the moonshine drinkers and gamblers and the sports and the fancy women usually gathered enjoying their own good time between the innings as much as the game itself.

Sometimes the dance orchestras, which were called social bands and ragtime bands and jazz bands but never blues bands or orchestras, also used to play at picnics and at baseball games, especially when it was also a holiday such as the Fourth of July or Labor Day, and afterwards at the dances in all the big ballrooms as well as all the honky-tonks. Because there were ballroom dances to celebrate every holiday of the year in addition to all the other special social occasions not sponsored by the church.

There were also the traveling minstrels and the vaudeville shows in those days. They used to stop and play the villages and small towns en route to the next big city theater for the next weekend. And sometimes when they pulled in early enough they also used to send the orchestra around on a truck, with the upright piano jangling and tinkling behind the driver's cabin, the slide trombone tiger-ragging out through the tailgate opening, with the woodwinds doubling in the background and the trumpet climbing up and up and away, echoing across the rooftops and steeples and all the way out beyond the trees to the hills and the outlying regions. Sometimes there was also the singer whose picture was on the advance placards pasted up all over town, especially if it was somebody like, say, Ma Rainey, Ida Cox, Bessie, Clara, Mamie, or Trixie Smith, but singers were mostly to be seen and anticipated, while the barker spieled the come-on through a megaphone.

The old downhome ragtime and barrelhouse piano players used to play (and more often than not, also sing) at night, because except for late Saturday afternoon and late Sunday afternoon that was when most people used to go to the honky-tonks during the week. So, when you were either not yet old enough to be allowed out that late, or you were too good a church member ever to be caught in such places, you heard the piano players mostly in the distance. But sometimes when business was good enough some of them also used to play during weekday afternoons and you could hear them from the street.

But the best time for honky-tonk piano players and blues singers back in those days was always Saturday night. Because the downhome workweek being what it was, that was when most people were out for a good time, and along with all the good barbecue and fried chicken, seafood, and all the whiskey and all the cigars and cigarettes and shaving lotions and hair pomade and

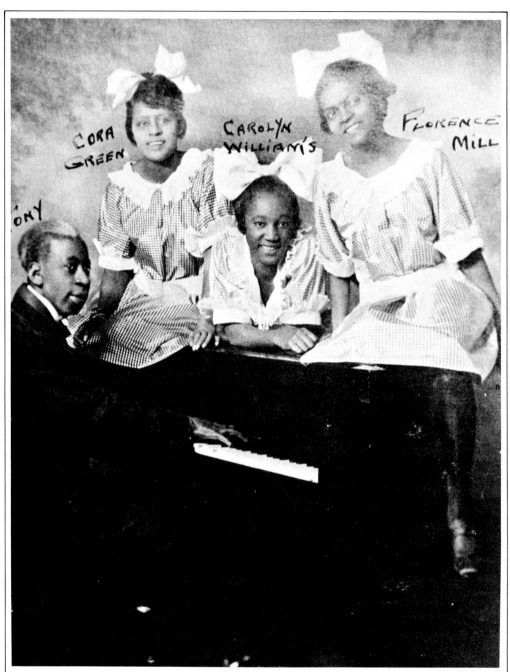

Tony Jackson, 1876–1921, by all accounts the most formidable of Storyville piano players, was also known as a great self-accompanied vocalist. According to Jelly Roll Morton, for whom he seemed to have been as legendary a figure as Buddy Bolden, "he enjoyed playing all classes of music in the style they was composed in, from blues to opera." Jackson went on tour with the Whitman Sisters' New Orleans Troubadours as a featured entertainer. From 1905 until his death his main base of operations was Chicago. Jackson's best-known compositions are *Pretty Baby, The Naked Dance,* and *Michigan Water Blues.*

Jelly Roll Morton, nine years younger than Tony Jackson, claimed to have studied under him. Like Jackson, he started as a self-accompanied singer working in the sporting houses of Storyville. Around 1904 he left New Orleans traveling mostly as a single attraction playing in honky-tonks. At Jackson's suggestion he went to Chicago in 1907 but didn't settle there. At other times he lived in New York and in California. He says he wrote his famous *Kansas City Stomp* not in Kansas City but in Tijuana, Mexico, while playing at the Kansas City Bar. Morton often gave the impression that he was as proud of being a city-slicking pool sharp as of being a great musician.

perfume and powder, almost everywhere you went there was also music for dancing, and it went on and on into the night and sometimes until daybreak Sunday morning.

So if what you were looking for was the kind of cozy rocking, cozy stomping, downhome good time that goes with the best low-down dirty mean back-alley blues music, there was no time like Saturday night and no place like the honky-tonks, which were also called jook joints and jook houses, when the right singers plus the right piano players (or guitar players) were on hand. But one thing about the honky-tonks was that they featured mostly what was essentially the familiar blues music all the time, much the same, come to think of it, as the Sunday Morning Service retained the traditional chants, moans, hymnbook hymns, anthems, spirituals, and gospel ballads over the years, new compositions being not so much a matter of experiment and innovation as of contribution in kind.

Another thing about the honky-tonks was the big risk you were always running just by being anywhere near them. There was no admission fee; but not only were they forever being raided, broken up either by the county sheriff and his deputies or by the city police, there was also no telling when somebody was going to start another knock-down drag-out rumpus, or there would be another cutting scrape, or the bullets would start flying again. Because the music always added up to a good-time atmosphere. But not for everybody. For some, acceleration of the festivities only aggravated their torment, especially when the object of their passion was their having a good time with somebody else. What with the piano thumping and ringing and the singer walking it and talking it like an evangelist at a revival meeting, somebody was always getting *besides* himself and somebody else was forever getting maimed for life or killed right on the spot.

Saturday night was also the best time to hear the dance bands in such ballrooms as the Elks' Lodge, the Masonic Temple, Odd Fellows' Hall, the Casino, the Pavillion, and the like, where the pay dances and the private invitational socials were held. That was when you could find not only most of the local bands playing somewhere, but as often as not also a territory band or two. And that was also when the long-range traveling bands advertised on the placards were most likely to be booked for, although when

Stomping on Blue. The variations are endless.

they were famous enough and there was notice far enough in advance they were booked for any night their itinerary permitted.

The next best time for all the local bands, nearby territory bands, and also the road bands was on Friday nights. Because during nine months of the year, that was when most of the school-sponsored public dances were scheduled in the big ballrooms, as were also such annual dress-up and costume balls as did not fall on such holidays as Halloween, Saint Valentine's Day, Mardi Gras, Fourth of July, and Labor Day.

Also, the ballroom dances were where you used to hear the ballad singers as well as the blues singers (who were sometimes both), with the ballroom orchestras almost always playing some of the current popular hit tunes and some of their own arrangements and compositions as well as some of the usual everyday twelve-bar blues. Because there were always some dancers who wanted to do all of the latest steps plus all the standard ballroom steps, including at least one waltz, as well as some honky-tonk back-alley shuffling and rolling if the occasion permitted.

Then along with all the phonograph records, there were also the radio networks broadcasting dance music as well as popular songs and concert music day and night, and in no time at all there were more blues-oriented dance bands on the road than ever before. Because whatever else it was used for it was always mostly dance music. Even when it was being performed as an act in a variety show on a vaudeville stage, the most immediate and customary response consisted of such foot tapping, hand clapping, body rocking, and hip rolling as came as close to total dance movement as the facilities and the occasion would allow. Nor was the response likely to be anything except more of the same when the most compelling lyrics were being delivered by Ma Rainey or Bessie Smith, whose every stage gesture, by the way, was also as much dance movement as anything else.

Because such dance steps as consisted of bumping and bouncing, dragging and stomping, hopping and jumping, rocking and rolling, shaking and shouting, and the like, were (and are) precisely what all the percussive incantation was (and still is) all about in the first place; and obviously such movements add up to a good time regardless of the lyrics. Purification and celebration/affirmation without a doubt. But not because the participants proceed in

138

such terms. So far as they are concerned they are out for a good time, which of course is not only reason enough but turns out to be the same thing in any case. And besides, aren't the most functional rituals precisely those that have long since become the most casual conventional and customary procedures?

All the same, it is the symbolical and ceremonial aspects of honky-tonk and ballroom dancing that downhome churchfolk object to first of all. They condemn all the good-time slow dragging, belly rubbing, hip grinding, flirtatious strutting, shouting, and stomping expressly because they regard such movements as not only sinful acts, but sinful ceremony to boot, which they seem to be clearly convinced is even worse. Indeed the impression of honky-tonk dancing that downhome churchfolk have given over the years is that it amounts to the breaking of all the Ten Commandments together.

Nothing therefore is more misleading than the standard dictionary emphasis on gloomy lyrics, the so-called blue notes, and slow tempo—as if blues music were originally composed to be performed as concert music, if not at a prayer meeting or at a convention of beggars. But just as the downhome church elders know better, so do the dance-hall patrons, not to mention working musicians, to whom *it don't mean a thing if it ain't got that swing* was a basic everyday operating principle long before the so-called Swing Era.

What W. C. Handy once wrote about the first performance of one of the great standards contains a typical account of the practical concerns of a working blues composer. "When *The St. Louis Blues* was written," he reports in his autobiography,

> the tango was in vogue. I tricked the dancers by arranging a tango introduction, breaking abruptly into a low-down blues. My eyes swept the floor anxiously, then suddenly I saw the lightning strike. The dancers seemed electrified. Something within them came suddenly to life. An instinct that wanted so much to live, to fling its arms and to spread joy, took them by their heels. By this I was convinced that my new song was accepted.

About the words, Handy, who was his own lyricist, had already written that he had

> decided to use Negro phraseology and dialect. I felt then, as I feel now, that this often implies more than well-chosen English can

139

> briefly express. My plot centered around the wail of a lovesick woman for her lost man, but in the telling of it I resorted to the humorous spirit of the bygone coon songs. I used the folk blues three-line stanza that created the twelve-measure strain.

He traces the germinal idea for his composition back to one night when he heard a drunken woman stumbling along a dimly lighted street in St. Louis mumbling, "My man's got a heart like a rock cast in the sea." He remembers the key of G as having been derived from someone whom he had heard giving the figure calls for a dance known as the Kentucky breakdown in a voice like a Presiding Elder preaching at a revival meeting. Then he goes on to say:

> My aim would be to combine ragtime syncopation with a real melody in the spiritual tradition. There was something in the Tango I wanted too. The dancers had convinced me that there was something racial in their response to this rhythm and I had used it in a disguised form in *The Memphis Blues*. Indeed the very word "tango" as I now know, was derived from the African "tangura," and signified this same tom-tom beat. This would figure in my introduction as well as in the middle strain.

Handy, who in 1912 had published *The Memphis Blues*, which he says caused people to dance in the streets in 1909, was recalling 1914. Jelly Roll Morton, the influence of whose musicianship has been infinitely greater than Handy's, says he called a composition he wrote in 1905 in tribute to Porter King, a fellow honky-tonk piano player, *The King Porter Stomp* because it made people stomp their feet. Freddie Keppard's direction to the musicians playing with him was always the same: "Let me hear the feet. Let me hear the feet."

And already before Handy or Morton or Bunk Johnson, Freddie Keppard, and King Oliver, there was the heyday of Buddy Bolden, whose dance-beat orientation went all the way back to the last days of the ancestral dances in Congo Square. The only existing photograph of him shows him and his sextet in a standard band pose for camera, with him holding his cornet chest-high. But the image that always comes first to mind is of him as the Pied Piper of New Orleans dancers; which is also how Jelly Roll Morton, who was there, recollects him:

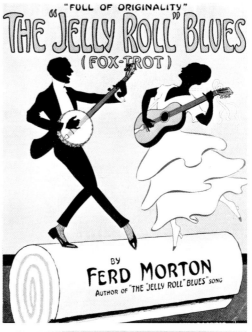

(Left) Freddie Keppard, 1889–1933, was in his prime from 1905 until the mid-twenties. Legend has it that he turned down the opportunity to be the first of the great New Orleans trumpet/cornet players to record because he was afraid that records would make it too easy for other musicians to imitate his style. (Bottom, right) Jelly Roll Morton, who first heard Keppard in 1907 and played with him in New Orleans in 1908, once said of him that "He hit the highest and the lowest notes on a trumpet that anybody outside of Gabriel ever did. He had the best tone, the best ear, and the most marvelous execution I ever heard and there was no end to his ideas…"

I remember we'd be hanging around some corner, wouldn't know that there was going to be a dance out at Lincoln Park. Then we'd hear old Buddy's trumpet coming on and we'd all start. Any time it was quiet at night at Lincoln Park because maybe the affair hadn't been so well publicized, Buddy Bolden would publicize it! He'd turn his trumpet around toward the city and blow his blues, calling his children home, as he used to say.

The old saying which Duke Ellington turned into a popular tune (and also into a catch phrase for a generation in the bargain) was not so much a statement of fact as a declaration of working principles. *Music* which is not sufficiently dance-beat oriented is not likely to be received with very much enthusiasm by the patrons of downhome honky-tonks, uptown cabarets, and the ballrooms and casinos across the nation. Music can be sweet (and low and ever so slow), or it can be hot (and also fortissimo and up up-tempo) so long as it has the idiomatic rhythmic emphasis that generates the dance-step response. In other words, the incantation must be so percussion oriented that it disposes the listeners to bump and bounce, to slow-drag and steady shuffle, to grind, hop, jump, kick, rock, roll, shout, stomp, and otherwise swing the blues away.

Ellington, who at the time was well on the way to become the outstanding arranger/composer and maestro of the idiom, but was anything but pontifical about anything, was probably only declaring his own definitive aesthetic position, which he never abandoned. Even such extended recital pieces as *Black, Brown and Beige* (RCA Victor LPM 1715), *Such Sweet Thunder* (Columbia CL 1033), *A Tone Parallel to Harlem* [*Harlem*] (RCA Victor LJM 1002), *Suite Thursday* (Columbia CS 8397), are dance-beat oriented; and so are his *Sacred Concerts* (RCA Victor LSP 3582; Fantasy 8407/8; RCA Victor APL 1-0785), which were oratorios written to be performed not in a Holy Roller Church down home but in such all but totally restrained precincts of the Sunday Morning Service as Grace Cathedral, in San Francisco; Fifth Avenue Presbyterian Church and St. John the Divine, in New York; the Church of Saint Sulpice, in Paris; and Coventry Cathedral and

●

(Preceding spread) Buddy Bolden, 1868–1931, (standing second from right) and his band, in the early 1890s. He was the epic hero not only of trumpet players but also of blues-oriented instrumentalists and dance-band leaders as well. During his heyday he is said to have had as many as seven bands all playing in different New Orleans dance halls at the same time, and used to make the rounds with his solo cornet keeping the festivities at the proper pitch of merriment as if with a magic wand.

Duke Ellington, for whom the *sine qua non* of composition was the dance-hall situation. (Following spread) A party in Chicago in honor of Ellington and Armstrong (fifth and sixth from left) in 1935.

PART
DUKE ELLI
AT T
F

FEDERAL BUILDING

TA...

...NOR OF
...AND LOUIS ARMSTRONG
...TAVERN - 51 - W - 31ST STREET
1935 - CHICAGO - ILL.

Westminster Abbey, in England. Indeed, some thirty-odd years after *It Don't Mean a Thing if It Ain't Got that Swing*, Ellington was to say: "We've done things with the symphony orchestras and our major effort has been to make the symphony orchestra swing, which everybody says can't be done, but I think we managed to do it very well."

But, despite the very strong likelihood that Ellington was mainly speaking of his own conception of blues music, the old saying which he set to music was also a very appropriate motto for the aesthetic point of view that Louis Armstrong, Promethean bringer of syncopated lightning from the Land of the Titans that he was, seems to have taken for granted from the very outset, and to which musicians across the nation (including Ellington himself) were converted in multitudes as if by a spellbinding evangelist. Thus it was also as if Ellington, whose music embodies among other things the most comprehensive synthesis of Armstrong's innovations, was declaring that for most intents and purposes the Armstrong Principle was universal.

Kansas City
Four/Four
and the
Velocity of
Celebration

Nowhere else in the nation and at no other time have blues musicians ever been more firmly dedicated to the proposition that it don't mean a thing if it ain't got that swing than in Kansas City in the early 1930s. Nor was the result of the dedication of this group of journeymen and apprentices to remain primarily a matter of local interest for very long. In no time at all riffing traditional blues choruses in medium- or up-tempo in a steady pulsing Kansas City Four/Four beat was picked up by musicians elsewhere as if it had been in the public domain all along, and was soon to become and remain the fail-safe tactic used by blues musicians across the nation on all occasions for calling Buddy Bolden's Children home to the good-time downhome ambiance of the Saturday Night Function.

Sometimes when Jo Jones (*né* Jonathan David), who was there from Birmingham, Alabama, by way of the entertainment circuit, remembers how things were in Kansas City back in those days, it is as if the whole town was one big music workshop. Some places never closed, he has told more than one interviewer, "You could be sleeping one morning at six A.M.., and a traveling band would come into town for a few hours, and they would wake you up to make a couple of hours' session with them until eight in the morning. You never knew what time in the morning someone would knock on your door and say they were jamming down the street."

Mary Lou Williams, who was also there (from Pittsburgh and also by way of the meandering route of the road musician) remembers things in much the same way. When she arrived to join her

151

husband, John Williams, a reedman in Andy Kirk's band at the Pla-Mor Ballroom, she found music all over town and musicians from everywhere, and there was also plenty of fine barbecue and seafood. There was always somewhere to go and hear music, and in addition to the regular cabarets and ballrooms, there were jam sessions all the time; and sometimes as many as twelve bands would take turns playing during the annual big shindig sponsored by the local musician's union. And along with such unforgettable piano players as Sammy Price, Pete Johnson, Clyde Hart, and the then young Count Basie, she also found three women, Julia Lee, who achieved a measure of national recognition as a singer as well; one she remembers only as Oceola; and another known as Countess Margaret.

Count Basie was there from Red Bank, New Jersey, by way of the vaudeville route. Andy Kirk was there from Denver, Colorado, by way of Texas and Oklahoma with The Clouds of Joy (once T. Holder's then his). Walter Page was there from Gallatin, Missouri, by way of Oklahoma City and the Blue Devils Orchestra, Hot Lips Page and Buster Smith were there from Texas by way of Oklahoma City and the same Blue Devils. And so was Lester Young, from Mississippi and Louisiana, by way of the Southwest minstrel, circus, and medicine-show circuit plus the territorial bands, including the Blue Devils.

Very much there already, and long since a part of what getting there was all about for the others was Bennie Moten, whose orchestra (which already had a reputation that extended beyond the region) was later to include a number of Blue Devils and after his sudden death would become the nucleus of the great Count Basie Orchestra. Also already there during that time were the bands of George E. Lee, Clarence Love, and Chauncey Downs (known as the Rinky Dinks).

There were such ballrooms as the Pla-Mor, the Fairyland Park, the Frog Hop in nearby St. Joseph; and such fabulous night spots as the Cherry Blossom, the Reno Club, from which the new Count Basie Orchestra was to be heard on radio in 1936; and Piney Brown's Sunset Club at 12th Street and Highland, where Pete Johnson used to play piano and Big Joe Turner used to shout the blues and serve drinks at the same time. There was also Piney Brown's Subway Club, at 18th and Vine, where so many newcom-

(Top) Mary Lou Williams was already a piano player of considerable professional experience when she went to Kansas City. As a member of Andy Kirk's Clouds of Joy she established a nationwide reputation via radio and records as an outstanding performer and a significant arranger /composer as well. (Bottom, left) Julia Lee, singer and piano player and sister of George E. Lee, was a native of Kansas City. (Bottom, right) Pete Johnson, also a native of Kansas City, was, along with Big Joe Turner, a mainstay of Kansas City night life. Later he also enjoyed wide popularity as a boogie-woogie piano player.

(Top) Andy Kirk directing the Clouds of Joy, with Mary Lou Williams, who was also one of the band's chief arrangers, at the piano. Other Clouds of Joy to achieve national popularity were Pha Terrell (seated) whose big hit was *Until the Real Thing Comes Along*; and Floyd Smith, (not in picture), who wrote and performed *Floyd's Guitar Blues*. Directly above the piano is Dick Wilson, the band's tenor-sax star. To his right is John Williams, who was then Mary Lou's husband. (Bottom) The George E. Lee Orchestra, with George (third from left) and young Julia (center), was at one time the main territorial business competition for the Bennie Moten Orchestra. The Lees were part of a family of professional musicians well known throughout the Kansas City area.

(Top) The Thirteen Original Blue Devils, with Lester Young and Buster Smith (back row, third and fourth from left), were "original" Blue Devils in name only in 1932, the date of the picture. They were preceded by Walter Page's Blue Devils of 1929–30 (bottom). According to Page, holding trumpet, who is said to have organized the Blue Devils as a territory band operating out of Oklahoma City some time earlier, the line-up of the first Blue Devils (not shown) was James Simpson, Jimmy LuGrand, and Oran "Hot Lips" Page, trumpets; Eddie Durham and somewhat later Dan Minor, trombones; Buster Smith, Reuben Roddy, and Ted Manning, reeds; Reuben Lynch, guitar; Turk Thomas, piano; Alvin Burroughs, drums; with Page himself playing baritone, tuba, and bass violin. Basie and Rushing joined in 1928 and left for the Moten band in 1929.

ers got their first local exposure, and also where ambitious youngsters got a chance to sit in with the established professionals, which was also the way it was at the Yellow Front Saloon when it was run by Ellis (The Chief) Burton as if as much for the benefit of the musicians as for the entertainment of the paying customers.

It was a good-time town where a lot of people went out to eat and drink and socialize every night. So there were big bands as well as combos, quartets, trios, and accompanied soloists working somewhere all during the week as well as Fridays and Saturdays and holidays; and when on special occasions the big ballrooms and outdoor pavilions used to sponsor a battle of the bands as an added feature, the excitement, anticipation, and partisanship would be all but indistinguishable from that generated by a championship boxing match or baseball game.

The band to beat back in the old days was always the one led by Bennie Moten, who because of his emphasis on high-level musicianship and all-round classiness was sometimes called the Duke Ellington of the West. Members of the old Blue Devils Orchestra brag about winning so many battles against so many other bands that Bennie Moten not only would not do battle with them, but as a matter of historical fact, hired away most of their best members, beginning with Count Basie, Eddie Durham, Jimmy Rushing, Hot Lips Page, and eventually including Walter Page and Buster Smith. Members of The Rockets still tell about how after leaving Moten upon the arrival of so many Blue Devils they later got the best of him in the annual battle of the bands.

The Kansas City jam sessions, whose influence on most contemporary blues musicianship has been far more direct than, say, the old New Orleans street parades, were already a matter of legend and myth even then. Most often mentioned are the ones at the Sunset, the Subway, the Reno, and the Cherry Blossom. But as almost everybody who was there remembers it now, since there

●

(Preceding page) Bennie Moten at the Fairyland Park in 1931 (Back row, left to right) Bennie Moten, Ira "Buster" Moten, and Jimmie Rushing. (Front row, left to right) Vernon Page, bass horn; William (later, Count) Basie, piano; Hot Lips Page, trumpet; Ed Lewis, trumpet; Thamon Hayes, trombone; Eddie Durham, trombone, guitar, arranger; Woody Walder, reeds; Leroy Berry, banjo; Harlan Leonard, reeds; Booker Washington, trumpet; Willie McWashington, drums; Jack Washington, reeds, including baritone. In addition to Basie, Rushing, Durham, and Hot Lips Page, the Moten roster was also to include such ex–Blue Devils as Walter Page, Buster Smith, Lester Young, and Dan Minor. Eddie Durham played a key role in the evolution of the style of the Count Basie orchestra from the Blue Devils and the Bennie Moten band.

(Top, left) Buster Smith became one of the leaders of the Blue Devils when Walter Page was hired by Bennie Moten. (Top, right) Ben Webster, 1909–73, a native of Kansas City, played with the Clouds of Joy, Bennie Moten, and also with Fletcher Henderson, among others; but is most widely celebrated for his performances with Duke Ellington, especially on *Cotton Tail, C-Jam Blues, All Too Soon, Blues Serge, Raincheck, Just a-Settin' and a-Rockin'*, and *Johnny Come Lately*. (Bottom, left) Herschel Evans with Lester Young delivered the one-two tenor-sax punch in the sensational Count Basie band of 1936–39. As on *One o'Clock Jump, Let Me See*, and *Doggin' Around*. Evans usually but not always made the hot getaway or set-up tenor statement, and Young made the cool wrap-up, clean-up, or knockout before the outchorus. (Bottom, right) Dick Wilson was one of the top resident tenor-sax contenders likely to be encountered in a jam session at any time in Kansas City before the Clouds of Joy left town.

159

FULL-RANGE
RECORDING

Vocalion

5118
(25297)

LESTER LEAPS IN
Fox Trot -Young-
COUNT BASIE
KANSAS CITY SEVEN

Lester Young and Coleman Hawkins (inset) are the two great touchstones of the blues-idiom tenor-sax statement. It was Hawkins, five years Young's senior, who established the tenor as a major solo voice among other instruments featured by blues musicians. In a sense, Young consolidated Hawkin's achievement by giving the tenor voice a strikingly different instrumental dimension. In contrast to Hawkins, who played with a big tone, pronounced vibrato, and whose virtuoso technique was all but overwhelming, Young, who had Herschel Evans, a Hawkins-style tenor man, at hand to counterstate every night in the Basie reed section, played with a considerably lighter tone and almost no vibrato; somehow his matchless virtuosity always came across as a matter of individuality rather than technique.

In all of Lester Young's finest solos (as in Ellington's always ambivalent foxtrots) there are overtones of unsentimental sadness that suggest that he was never unmindful of human vulnerability and was doing what he was doing with such imperturbable casualness not only in spite of but also as a result of all the trouble he had seen, been beset by, and somehow survived. In a sense, the elegance of earned self-togetherness and with-it-ness so immediately evident in all his quirky lyricism is the musical equivalent of the somewhat painful but nonetheless charismatic parade-ground strut of the

162

campaign-weary soldier who has been there one more time and made it back in spite of hell and high water with shrapnel exploding all around him. A typical Lester Young solo on an up-tempo number, especially one of the now classic Basie recordings, is as symbolic of heroic action as any fairy-tale exploit.

was a piano (and as often as not, a set of drums also) in almost every joint, there was no telling when or where the next one would get going. Nor was there ever any telling when one would break up. It was quite common for musicians to improvise on one number for more than an hour at such times, and sometimes the session would run well into the next day—as happened the time Coleman Hawkins came to town with the Fletcher Henderson Orchestra and got hung up at the Cherry Blossom with Hershel Evans, Ben Webster, Dick Wilson, and Herman Wadler, among others, including Lester Young, who was not only to achieve a status as tenor saxophonist comparable to that of Hawkins himself, theretofore the undisputed master, but was also to be considered an innovator of perhaps even greater significance.

Sometimes these sessions turned into battles royal or "cutting" contests with the soloists trying to outdo each other; and sometimes they also served as showcases for new talent; but mostly the musicians just wanted to play for the sheer enjoyment of playing. Many musicians used to drop in to such places as the Sunset or the Subway on the way home from their regular engagements and end up jamming for nothing (except treats) the rest of the night. Because that was also where you could try out some of your own new ideas, and of course, it was absolutely the best way to keep current with the latest innovations. The number of Kansas City arrangements and compositions derived from jam sessions is incalculable.

Nor was the Kansas City jam session any less dance-beat oriented for being an experimental laboratory. Thus as much as the instrumental dueling at such sessions was to become a matter of storybook romance, what Kansas City musicians are most widely celebrated for is the drive with which they swing the blues and anything else in all tempos. Whatever they play becomes good-time music because they always maintain the velocity of celebration. Nothing's too fast or too slow to swing, runs Count Basie's correlative to the Armstrong/Ellington Principle: and in addition to the output of Basie's own orchestras over the years, there are also the collected works of Charlie Parker, perhaps the most workshop-oriented of all Kansas City apprentices, to bear him out in spite of all the undanceable European concert-oriented pretentiousness that has been perpetrated by self-styled disciples while using his name in vain. What you hear when you listen to

164

Charlie Parker was born in Kansas City in 1920 and so came of age during the so-called swing era in a town teeming with first-rate saxophone players. Parker's own dazzling innovations, a primal source of the so-called bop movement, were, unlike the clichés of most of his hypnotized imitators, the result of carefully nourished blues-idiom musicianship, brilliant conception, and authentic passion.

BILLIES BOUNCE
(Charles Parker)
CHARLEY PARKER'S REE BOPPERS
Charles Parker, alto sax; Miles Davis, trumpet; Curley Russell, bass; Hen Gates, piano; Max Roach, drums
573-A
(SAV-5850)
NOT LICENSED FOR RADIO BROADCAST · FOR HOME USE ON PHONOGRAPHS

165

Charlie Parker as a Kansas City innovator is not a theorist dead set on turning dance music into concert music. What you hear is a brilliant protégé of Buster Smith and admirer of Lester Young adding a new dimension of elegance to the Kansas City drive, which is to say to the velocity of celebration. Whether you listen to *Ko-Ko, Warming Up a Riff* (Savoy MG 12014); *Parker's Mood, Billie's Bounce* (Savoy MG 12009); *Charlie Parker with Strings* (Columbia 33 CX 10081 England); *KC Blues* (Verve V6-8409) or just anything chosen at random, the evidence is the same: Kansas City apprentice-become-master that he was, Charlie Parker was out to swing not less but more. Sometimes he tangled up your feet but that was when he sometimes made your insides dance as never before. At his best he could make your insides cut all the steps that your feet could not cut anyway.

Sometimes, as the traditional choreography of Saturday Night Function makes manifest, you get rid of the blues by jumping them, stomping them, swinging them (as a sack of rubbish), and so on. The special drive of Kansas City music is in this sense a device for herding or even stampeding the blues away. In any case the Kansas City drummer not only maintains that ever steady yet always flexible transcontinental locomotivelike drive of the KC 4/4, he also behaves for all the world like a whip-cracking trail driver. And so do Kansas City brass ensembles on occasion also bark and yap and snap precisely as if in pursuit of some invisible quarry, with the piano player sicking them on.

Similarly, as is altogether consistent with the characteristic velocity of affirmation and celebration that seems so inherent in the KC 4/4, the Kansas City blues singer, whose archetypes are Jimmy Rushing and Big Joe Turner, shouts the blues away and shouts a church-rocking-stomping-jumping-shimmying good time into being in the process. Obviously the shout-style vocal suggests the whistle of a transcontinental locomotive highballing it across the great plains. Also, whether or not another western workaday source of stylization for the Kansas City shout is the traditional whooping and hollering of the range rider and the trail driver, there is no question about whether or not Jimmy Rushing and Big Joe Turner rode herd on the blue devils, spurring on the instrumental accompaniment as if from the saddle atop a quarter horse the while.

(Top, left) Oran "Hot Lips" Page, 1908–54, went to Kansas City by way of the Blue Devils to play with Bennie Moten. A fine trumpet soloist and vocalist, he is also remembered by KC musicians as a peerless inventor of jam-session riff-chorus figures. (Top, right) W. C. Handy's *Joe Turner Blues* refers neither to Big Joe Turner, the one-time singing bartender perhaps best known for *Piney Brown's Blues,* nor to Joe Turner the piano player but to one about whom there are various tall tales dating from the nineteenth century. (Bottom, left) Jimmie Rushing, 1903–72, achieved fame as vocalist with the Count Basie band in the thirties. (Bottom, right) A. C. Godley was one of the many first-rate Kansas City drummers who helped to put the KC 4/4 in the public domain.

168

Big Joe Turner, not to be confused with the legendary Joe Turner of W.C. Handy's *Joe Turner Blues* or with Joe Turner the stride-oriented piano player from Baltimore, has long been considered the Big Daddy of traditional blues shouters. A native of Kansas City, Turner, who began as a blues-singing bartender and became one of the most popular local after-hours attractions for musicians as well as regular night club patrons, delivers his lyrics like a tenor sax player in a Kansas City combo.

But as far as that goes, sometimes it is also as if each Kansas City musician were riding the blues as if astride a bucking bronco. And come to think of it, wasn't there something of the rodeo about the Kansas City jam session from the outset? The competition among the participants was as incidental to the challenge of the music itself as the competition among cowboys for rodeo prizes was to the elemental contest between man and the wild animal.

●

About the evolution of the Kansas City Four/Four, Jo Jones, who as the drummer in the Count Basie Orchestra from the mid-thirties through the early forties was largely responsible for extending it into the national domain, has said: "When Bennie Moten's two beat one and three rhythm and the two and four of Walter Page's Blue Devils came together in the Basie band, there was an even flow one-two-three-four." (Walter Page himself playing what came to be known as walking string bass, with Eddie Durham and later Freddie Greene chording on rhythm guitar, provided the anchor for the Basie rhythm section, as Jo Jones mostly subdued his snare and bass except to accentuate, and rode his high-hat cymbal as if whispering. Meanwhile there was also the also and the so forth and so on of talking drums plus tinkling and singing bells in Count Basie's own nothing-if-not-percussive piano.)

The Four/Four is a definitive element of the Kansas City process of stylization, and so is the use of jam-session-like riff choruses as a basic structural device. As is well known, many of the most enduring Kansas City compositions, which are essentially a sequence of such choruses (some alternating with solos, some used as background for solos, and some in call-and-response exchanges between solo and ensembles) began as head, or improvised, arrangements of jam-session renditions. Indeed, sometimes all the arranger/composer had to do was routine the order and limit the duration and number of exchanges.

The natural history of Count Basie's *One o'Clock Jump* is described by Buster Smith in an interview published in *Jazz Review* (Jan. 1962): "We were fooling around at the club and Basie was playing along in F. That was his favorite key. He yelled to me that he was going to switch to D Flat and for me to get something. I started playing that opening reed trumpet and Dan Minor thought up the trombone part. That was it—a 'head'."

ERRATA

THE LAST PARAGRAPH ON PAGE 170
SHOULD READ AS FOLLOWS:

The natural history of Count Basie's *One O'Clock Jump*, as described by Buster Smith in an interview with Dave Gazzaway for *Jazz Review*, represents a commonplace procedure: *"We were fooling around at the club and Basie was playing along in F. That was his favorite key. He hollered to me that he was going to switch to D Flat and for me to 'set' something. I started playing that opening reed riff [from Six or Seven Times] on alto. Lips Page jumped in with the trumpet part without any trouble and Dan Minor thought up the trombone part. That was it— a 'head.'"*

(Top) Dicky Wells, who had played with Elmer Snowden, Luis Russell, Benny Carter, Fletcher Henderson, and others, was added to the Basie trombone section in New York in 1938 and soon became one of the band's top soloists and one of the most instinctive instrumental voices in the idiom. (Bottom) Count Basie and key sidemen, circa 1937. Left to right, Eddie Durham, Herschel Evans, Benny Morton, Lester Young, and Buck Clayton.

Most of the early compositions that make up the now classic Basie repertory seem to have begun as head arrangements. As Dicky Wells, who was featured in the trombone section from 1938 to 1949, told Stanley Dance in *Night People*:

> Basie would start out and vamp a little, set a tempo and call out 'that's it!' He'd set a rhythm for the saxes first, and Earle Warren in Buster Smith's old alto seat would pick that up and lead the saxes. Then he'd set one for the bones and we'd pick that up. Now it's our rhythm against theirs. The third rhythm would be for the trumpets and they'd start fanning with their derbies. [Derbies were very effective with brass sections then, and it's too bad they're so little used now. Derby men like Lips Page, Sidney De Paris, and Harry Edison could always make your insides dance.] The solos would fall in be tween the ensembles, but that's how the piece would begin, and that's how Basie put his tunes together.

What Wells, who was not a Kansas City apprentice, by the way, goes on to say a few pages later, obviously has as much to do with Kansas City as with Count Basie nevertheless:

> Basie really began to get a book together when Ed Durham was in the band. Basie and Ed would lock up in a room with a little jug, and Basie would play the ideas and Ed would voice them. . . . After Durham left Basie began to buy different arrangements from the outside. Even so Basie always played a big part, because he would cut out what he didn't like, what wasn't Western style, just as he does today, until he got it swinging. . . . He always believed in making people's feet pat. . . . And he had that feeling for tempo. He'd start the band off, maybe fool around with the rhythm section for thirty-two bars, until he got it right . . . .

Eddie Durham, the guitarist-trombonist-arranger/composer, who was there from Texas back in the good old days of perpetual high times, and whose *Out the Window, Time Out,* and *Topsy* (Decca DXSB 7170) are almost always included in listings of the Best of Count Basie, says:

●

(Preceding page) Count Basie and his orchestra in 1940. (Left to right) Walter Page, bass; Basie; Buddy Tate, tenor sax; Jo Jones, drums; Freddy Greene, guitar; Tab Smith, alto sax; Buck Clayton, trumpet; Vic Dickenson, trombone; Jack W. Washington, baritone sax; Dickie Wells, trombone; Ed Lewis, trumpet; Harry "Sweets" Edison, trumpet; Lester Young, tenor sax; Dan Minor, trombone. Tate was the replacement for Herschel Evans, who died in 1939.

It was as if Count Basie edited the orchestrations for his repertoire of the 1930s to late 40s on the same principles of composition that Ernest Hemingway learned from the style sheet for prose writers at the *Kansas City Star* back in 1917: "Use short sentences. Use short first paragraphs. Use vigorous English. Be positive, not negative. Never use old slang . . . slang to be enjoyable must be fresh. Avoid the use of adjectives, especially such extravagant ones as splendid, gorgeous, grand, magnificent, etc." Basie stripped his own Harlem Stride–derived piano style down to the point that he could make *one note* swing!

Classic Basie: *Time Out,* which contains a four-bar Herschel Evans introduction to a Lester Young solo, also features Buck Clayton, Eddie Durham (electric guitar), Basie, and Earle Warren, *Topsy* features Buck Clayton, Jack Washington, Basie, and Herschel Evans. *Sent for You Yesterday and Here You Come Today,* one of the band's most popular Jimmie Rushing shout vocals, is a typical example of blues music counterstating negative lyrics. *Moten Swing,* the Kansas City Anthem, is credited to Bennie and Buster Moten, but was actually composed by Eddie Durham from the chords of *You're Driving Me Crazy.* Durham laid out to do so during a set backstage at the Pearl Theater in Philadelphia in 1931 because a ride-out number was needed for the finale.

Basie was always full of ideas, but you couldn't get him to stay still long enough to get them down. We'd be working together, him playing and me writing, and after a few bars he'd start getting restless. He just wanted to play it. And after he got famous he didn't care about writing at all anymore. I used to try to tell him they ought to get somebody to write up all that good stuff we'd been playing all that time, and he'd just say, "Aw, hell, they won't voice it right."

Incidentally, the context of the performance is the primary consideration underlying the length of riff-chorus compositions. They often begin with a vamp, and they usually end with an outchorus or tag; but the number of ensembles and solos in the main body of both the traditional twelve-bar blues and thirty-two-bar pop forms vary in accordance with the situation. In a jam session they may run on indefinitely, as in the old Mary Lou Williams story about dropping members of the Andy Kirk band off at the Sunset on the way from their regular nightly nine to twelve engagement at the Pla-Mor, and going on home to bathe and change clothes and coming back to find Pete Johnson still riffing the same tune, with some of the musicians from Kirk's band now participating in relays. Sometimes the main reason Kansas City musicians recall the time the local saxophone players jumped Coleman Hawkins is to tell about how Ben Webster had to go and get Mary Lou Williams out of bed at 4 A.M. the next morning because they had worn out all of the available piano players. Jo Jones said it was not at all unusual for a number to be jammed for an hour and a half in those days.

The duration of a ballroom rendition for the customary turn around the dance floor tends to be approximately three minutes, which is also the length of the standard thirty-two-bar popular song, which was also the length of standard phono records. Perhaps as a result—but for whatever reason—even though most 33⅓ RPM recordings contain almost forty-five minutes of music (twenty-plus minutes per side), they tend to be albums or collections in which most of the items are less than ten minutes in duration. Not that Kansas City arranger/composers have failed to take advantage of the LP, but even so what they have mostly done is to extend the old three-minute composition much the same as it was always extended in the jam session. Sometimes they simply increase the duration of each solo. Sometimes they add new riff choruses, and sometimes they merely increase the number of re-petitions of the same riffs. On some occasions the outchorus may be extended into an encore, or indeed several encores, depending on how many times the leader says *One more time*.

•

But whatever the circumstances of the performance, and what-ever the duration of any given selection, Kansas City music seems always to have been nothing if not something to pat your feet by. And such has been the influence that it has exercised on contem-porary sensibilities that not only has it now come to seem to be the most natural and irrepressible musical expression of down-to-earth merriment in the world, but also, whether the occasion is a ball-room dance, a night-club show, a concert recital, a jam session, or a record party in a living room, as soon as the Four/Four begins (sometimes along with the vamp and sometimes after it and some-times before it) and the first riff chorus gets going, the atmosphere changes so instantaneously that it is as if a Master of the Revels had suddenly interrupted the proceedings to command: *"Say now, hey now, that's all right about all that other carrying on and stuff, I say let the good times roll!"*

The Blues as
Dance Music

Sometimes you get the impression that many of the articles and books about blues music were written by people who assume that the very best thing that could happen to it would be for it to cease being dance-hall music and become concert-hall music. Over the years most of these writers themselves have been show-biz-oriented entertainment-page reporters and reviewers, whose contact with the workaday environment of blues musicians is somewhat similar to that of the movie reporter and reviewer with the world of movie actors. So much so in fact that many have spent a considerable amount of time grinding out movie-fan-magazine–type articles on the personal lives of the more prominent performers, whom they glamorize and condescend to at the same time.

Many also overlard their copy with downhome and uptown slang expressions, such as *dig* for *understand* and *appreciate*, *bad* for *excellent*, *taking care of business* for *performing in an outstanding manner*, and so on, as if to prove that their contact with the idiom is that of a very hip which is to say sophisticated insider. But sometimes the results are even more exasperating than ludicrous. Item: The use of the word *funky* to mean earthy and soulful. The insider's traditional use is synonymous with foul body odor and connotes the pungent smell of sweat-saturated clothes and unwashed bodies, undeodorized armpits, improperly wiped backsides, urine-stained and fart-polluted undergarments. To the ever-so-hip reporter *funky* seems to suggest earthy people-to-people euphoria. To the insider it suggests asphyxiation. As in a version of Jelly Roll Morton's *Buddy Bolden's Blues*:

I thought I heard Buddy Bolden say
Nasty, dirty, funky butt take him away.
I thought I heard Buddy Bolden shout
Open up the window and let the bad air out.

But with all their pseudo-inside wordplay, all the gratuitous redundancies about jazz which is to say blues music being an art form indigenous to the United States, and indeed with all their ever ready lip-service to the element of swing as a definitive factor of the idiom, when these very same reporter/reviewers give their evaluations of actual performances, whether live or on records, it is almost always as if they were writing about the concert music of Europe. They condone as well as condemn on assumptions that are essentially those of the European Academy. Not that they themselves seem to be basically hostile to any of the indispensable elements of the idiom. On the contrary, they seem to be personally fascinated and delighted by them. But even so they almost always write as if about concert-hall music rather than dance music.

Some have even written that blues musicians should not have to play in honky-tonks, dance halls, night clubs, variety shows, popular festivals, and the like. As if downright oblivious to the literal source as well as the intrinsic nature and function of the idiom, some have gone so far as to represent the experience of playing in Storyville, or the dives and dance halls of Memphis, Chicago, Kansas City, and Harlem as a most outrageous form of injustice! There are those who even as they used to declare Duke Ellington to be the greatest of American composers immediately began wringing their hands and shaking their heads over what struck them as being the cruel state of affairs that forced him to spend most of his time on the road with his orchestra playing in night clubs, ballrooms, and theaters. The fact that Duke Ellington had already become Ellington the Composer by writing music for such places long before his first Carnegie Hall concert seems to have escaped them at such moments, as did the fact that as important as formal concerts came to be to Ellington, he never expressed any desire to take his orchestra off the circuit. As he said one night during an intermission in a dance at the Propeller Club at Tuskegee to a young literary type who was concerned about an article that had

182

reported him (Ellington) as having said that he continued to write dance music mainly to win more people over to his longer concert pieces:

> Don't pay any attention to those guys, sweetie. When you get so goddamn important you can't play places like this anymore you might as well give it up, because you're finished. We try to play everything. We're always very happy when they ask us to play proms, weddings, country clubs, ballparks. You see, this way we get to have most of the fun, because the dancers are not just sitting there watching; they're having a ball.

There is nothing at all ironic about *Stomping at the Savoy* and *Moten Swing* being written by musicians for whom the Saturday Night Function was as much a part of what life is all about as is the Sunday Morning Service. Nor does there seem to be any compelling reason why the audiences for whom such music was written and performed in the first place should not continue to be able to enjoy it in its natural setting simply because another audience now exists in the concert hall.

Not that the function of the concert hall is not also fundamental. It provides a showcase for the new and serves as a permanent gallery, so to speak, for the enduring. Moreover, as in the case of the great masterpieces of European church music, it affords opportunities for the music to be heard on its own apart from its role as an element in a ritual, in other words as a work of art per se. Thus the concert-hall recital at its best is in a very real sense also an indispensable extension of the dance hall. It can serve as a sort of finger-snapping, foot-tapping annex auditorium, where the repertory includes not only the new and the perennial but also such classics as, say, *Grandpa's Spells, Sugar Foot Stomp,* and *Potato Head Blues*, that some dancers may be too fad-conditioned or otherwise preoccupied to request. Also, inasmuch as all occasions and circumstances seem to generate musical responses sooner or later, there is nothing intrinsically inauthentic about blues music which is composed specifically for concert recital.

But then the phonograph record has served as the blues musician's equivalent to the concert hall almost from the outset. It has been in effect his concert hall without walls, his *musée imaginaire*, his comprehensive anthology, and also his sacred repository and official archive. Many blues-idiom composers use the recorded

183

performance as the authorized score. Jo Jones and Eddie Durham have said that the first written arrangement of Count Basie's *One o'Clock Jump* was copied from the record by Buck Clayton (Decca DXSB 7170). Historians and critics of the idiom also use the recorded performance as the official score. What Martin Williams, for example, refers to in his discussion of Jelly Roll Morton, Duke Ellington, and Thelonious Monk as outstanding composers is not their collected scores but their recorded performances. Williams's book *The Jazz Tradition* is based primarily on recorded performances, and the same is true of Gunther Schuller's *Early Jazz*.

Nor is that all. For much goes to show that it may have been precisely the phonograph record (along with radio) that in effect required the more ambitious blues musicians to satisfy the concert-oriented listeners and Bacchanalian revelers at the very same time; long before the first formal concerts. Even as Chick Webb kept them stomping at the Savoy Ballroom on Lenox Avenue in Harlem, and Earl Hines kept them shuffling at the Grand Terrace on the South Side in Chicago, their orchestras were also playing what to all intents and purposes was a finger-snapping, foot-tapping concert for listeners huddled around radios all over the nation. (Not a few dance parties all over the nation were also geared to the radio, but that is another story.) Moreover most of the program was either already available on records or soon would be. When any of the orchestras that had made recordings of merit went on tour, musicians found other musicians and laymen alike in almost every town who were not only as familiar with their styles as with the mannerisms of a favorite athlete but also could recite their solos note for note.

Anytime a band pulled into town early enough before the engagement it was always the same story no matter where it was: *"Hey, here's that Goddamn Lester, man. Goddamn. What say Lester? This my man, cousin. Dogging Around, man, you know that record? That's my record. Right after old Count gets through cutting his little old diamond, here come my natural boy: Doo dooby dooby dooby daba doodadoo . . . . Say what you drinking Lester? You want something to eat? You can't spend no money in this town, Lester. You know that, don't you?*

"Man, here that bad Mr. Johnny Hodges. Man, here the Rabbit, in person all the way from the Cotton Club in the Heart of Harlem.

184

Chick Webb and his Savoy Ballroom orchestra with
Ella Fitzgerald. Titles in the Webb repertoire that fulfill
the requirements of dancers, radio audiences, and record players at the same time include: *Stomping at the
Savoy, Don't Be That Way, If Dreams Come True, Blue
Lou, Liza, In the Groove at the Grove, Let's Get Together, Undecided,* and *Blue Minor.*

185

Johnny Hodges, 1906-70, was one of the two greatest alto-saxophone players of all time. Indeed, he and Charlie Parker were to the alto what Coleman Hawkins and Lester Young were to the tenor. On some compositions Hodges functioned in effect as Ellington's instrumental extension of Bessie Smith. His unsurpassed soulfulness is as much in evidence on such small-combo numbers as *Good Queen Bess* and *Going Out the Back Way*, as on full-band classics like *I Let a Song Go Out of My Heart* and *Don't Get Around Much Anymore*, or such slow melodic mood pieces as *Warm Valley* and *Day Dream*.

BLUEBIRD

"HIS MASTER'S VOICE"
REG. U. S. PAT OFF   MARCA REGISTRADA

For best results use
RCA Victor Needles

B-11447-B

SQUATY ROO–Fox Trot
(Johnny Hodges)
Johnny Hodges and Orchestra
(An Ellington Unit)

RCA VICTOR DIVISION OF RADIO CORPORATION OF AMERICA, CAMDEN, N.J. MADE IN U.S.A.

186

Lester Young, also known as Prez, as in President, and bandstand audience. Although Young never became popular with the general public, his admirers—who include many musicians—were and are intensely loyal and remarkably enduring. Devotees of Armstrong and Ellington seem fairly well reconciled to the fact that they must share their idols with the world at large, including millions of squares. But many Lester Young fans seem to regard him as personal property to be shared only with other true believers.

DECCA

MANUFACTURED 'N U S A · BY DECCA RECORDS, INC.

(63920)   Fox Trot

DOGGIN' AROUND
(Herschel Evans)

COUNT BASIE
And His Orchestra

1965 B

*Hey, Johnny, you know that thing you did called Squaty Roo?
Man I played that record and some cats around here started to
give up blowing. Then they borrowed my record and like to wore it
out. You got them working, Johnny."*

Louis Armstrong had so many musicians working like that on his
records in so many places that people used to say all he had to do
to play a dance in any town of any size was just turn up with his
horn, because all he needed was a couple of hours and he could
round up enough local musicians who knew his records note for
note to make up any kind of band he wanted to work with for the
occasion. They also used to like to tell about how sometimes when
the people got there and saw all the hometown musicians on the
bandstand they started grumbling, and then old Louis would
thread it all together with his trumpet as if with a golden needle
and everybody would settle down and have a good time. Whether
that part was true or not the way they used to like to tell it, you
could see old Louis with his trumpet case and his manager with a
briefcase, and maybe a piano player with a folder full of music,
being met at the local train station in the middle of the afternoon
by the hometown promoter, who already had all the musicians
waiting for him at the dance hall. Then, as they used to tell it, all
old Louis would do was sit off to one side on the bandstand stripping and cleaning his horn piece by piece while the piano player
held the audition and ran through a quick rehearsal. That was all it
usually took, because what happened was that they spent the
whole dance playing for old Louis, while the rest of the local
musicians (along with a number of radio and record fans and
hipsters) clustered around the stage in what Count Basie has referred to as the bandstand audience and which is the ballroom
equivalent of the traditional Second Line that dances and prances
along beside the marching bands in the New Orleans street
parades.

In other words, although it may not have been possible for the
masterpieces of Mozart, Bach, and Beethoven to have been composed had not music been released from the restrictions of its
secondary role as an element in a ritual to become an independent
art form as such, it does not follow that the concert hall is therefore
indispensable to the extension, elaboration, and ultimate refinement of the intrinsic possibilities of blues music. For one thing, the

188

great body of European Art Music was already in existence and already a part of the heritage of blues musicians. It was already there to be played with, and blues musicians did just that, as they did with everything else in earshot that struck their fancy. And the dancers loved it.

But what is at issue is the primordial cultural conditioning of the people for whom blues music was created in the first place. They are dance-beat-oriented people. They refine all movement in the direction of dance-beat elegance. Their work movements become dance movements and so do their play movements; and so, indeed, do all the movements they use every day, including the way they walk, stand, turn, wave, shake hands, reach, or make any gesture at all. So, if the overwhelming preponderance of their most talented musicians has been almost exclusively preoccupied with the composition and performance of dance music, it is altogether consistent with their most fundamental conceptions of and responses to existence itself.

And besides, as little as has been made of it by students of culture, not to mention assessors and technicians of social well-being, the quality of dance music may actually be of far greater fundamental significance than that of concert music anyway. Dance, after all, not only antedates music, but is also probably the most specific source of music and most of the other art forms as well. It is not by chance that poetry, for instance, is measured in feet, and that drama was originally mainly a combination of poetry and choreography performed not on a stage but in the orchestra, in other words, a dancing place! Furthermore, dance, according to impressive anthropological data, seems to have been the first means by which human consciousness objectified, symbolized, and stylized its perceptions, conceptions, and feelings. Thus the very evidence which suggests that the pragmatic function of concert music is to represent the dancing of attitudes also serves to reinforce the notion that dance is indispensable.

●

Reporters and reviewers who assume that their role is to determine how well blues music measures up to standards based on principles formulated from the special conceptions and techniques of European concert-hall music are misguided not only as to the most pragmatic function of criticism but as to the fundamental

189

THE KING OF THE ZULU'S
(At A Chit'lin' Rag)
(Hardin)
LOUIS ARMSTRONG and his HOT FIVE

Louis Armstrong, also known as Satch or Satchmo, for Satchelmouth, erstwhile Dippermouth, wearing the mask of the King of the Zulus in the Mardi Gras parade, New Orleans, 1949. Many civil-rights spokesmen, for all their professed pride in their black African heritage, were downright scandalized when the long-since-world-renowned Armstrong declared that being chosen for such a role was the fulfillment of a lifelong dream. But perhaps they confused the ritual role of the Zulu King of Mardi Gras with that of minstrel entertainer. In any case they seem to have overlooked the fact (as a home-town boy would not) that the specific traditional ritual function of the outrageous costume and conduct of the King of the Zulus is to ridicule the whole idea of Mardi Gras and the Lenten season.

Louis Armstrong, as Pops (as he was known and re-vered among other blues musicians), in action. On the one hand he was an irrepressible comedian or satirist; on the other he was the Prometheus of the blues idiom. He arrived on the national scene from New Orleans as if from the land of the Titans, bringing with him the se-cret of making elegant figures with fire! Everywhere Armstrong went in the 1920s, he created a revolution in musical sensibility. Which is not to say that he in-vented the form but that his assimilation, elaboration, extensions, and refinement of its elements became in effect the touchstone for all who came after him. In-cidentally, for the most part Armstrong's comic mask, which as often as not was as much a matter of vocal inflection as mugging, was a convention for counter-stating sentimentality.

191

Armstrong as Culture Hero. So direct was his influence from the mid-twenties through the mid-thirties (by which time he had come to be taken for granted as a natural resource in the public domain) that other musicians not only memorized his records note for note and bought exercise books in order to approach his style through formal analysis and rehearsal but by the early thirties were also modeling their clothes on his. Special Armstrong sartorial details circa *When It's Sleepy Time Down South, Chinatown, Lazy River, I Got Rhythm, Wrap Your Troubles in Dreams, Stardust, Just a Gigolo, Shine:* a crisply ironed shirt with low-riding widespread collar worn with a smartly tailored three-piece suit and a tie with a large Windsor-type knot.

nature of art as well. For art is always a matter of idiomatic stylization, it transcends both time and place. Thus criticism, the most elementary obligation of which is to increase the accessibility of aesthetic presentation, is primarily a matter of coming to terms with such special peculiarities as may be involved in a given process of stylization.

What counts in a work of art, which after all must achieve such universality as it can through the particulars of the experience most native to it, is not the degree to which it conforms to theories, formulas, and rules that are best regarded as being, like Aristotle's *Poetics,* generalizations after the fact, but how adequately it fulfills the requirements of the circumstances for which it was created. When, as in the case of the masterpieces of Renaissance painting and Baroque music, great art goes beyond its original imperatives, it does so by extending the implications of its response to its original circumstances—as happened with the entertainments William Shakespeare concocted (in much the same manner as a blues-idiom arranger/composer, by the way) for the diversion of the patrons of the Globe Theatre. The source of the three unities in the drama of Ancient Greece is not Aristotle's abstractions about form and propriety but rather the vernacular circumstances of play production during the time of Aeschylus, Sophocles, and Euripides approximately a hundred years earlier!

Such being the nature of the creative process, the most fundamental prerequisite for mediating between the work of art and the audience, spectators, or readers, as the case may be, is not reverence for the so-called classics but rather an understanding of what is being stylized plus an accurate insight into how it is being stylized. Each masterwork of art, it must be remembered, is always first of all a comprehensive synthesis of all the aspects of its idiom. Thus to ignore its idiomatic roots is to miss the essential nature of its statement, and art is nothing if not stylized statement. Indeed it is precisely the stylization that is the statement. In short,

●

(Preceding spread) Traditional New Orleans marching and social band in action with its second-line dancing-and-prancing fans and protégés on the sidewalk. The size of the unit and tempo of the stride suggest that the band is ragging its way back into town from a cemetery service. En route to the cemetery the music is customarily solemn, but once the funeral is over the mood changes to playfulness and mockery. During big street parades such as are held at Mardi Gras time second liners are permitted to carry the instruments of their favorite musicians for several blocks while the band takes a breather before striking up again.

196

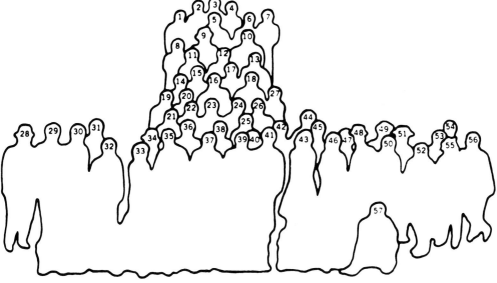

1. HILTON JEFFERSON; 2. BENNY GOLSON; 3. ART FARMER; 4. WILBUR WARE; 5. ART BLAKEY; 6. CHUBBY JACKSON; 7. JOHNNY GRIFFIN; 8. DICKIE WELLS; 9. BUCK CLAYTON; 10. TAFT JORDAN; 11. ZUTTY SINGLETON; 12. RED ALLEN; 13. TYREE GLENN; 14. MIFF MOLE; 15. SONNY GREER; 16. JAY C. HIGGINBOTHAM; 17. JIMMY JONES; 18. CHARLES MINGUS; 19. JO JONES; 20. GENE KRUPA; 21. MAX KAMINSKY; 22. GEORGE WETTLING; 23. BUD FREEMAN; 24. PEE WEE RUSSELL; 25. ERNIE WILKINS; 26. BUSTER BAILEY; 27. OSIE JOHNSON; 28. GIGI GRYCE; 29. HANK JONES; 30. EDDIE LOCKE; 31. HORACE SILVER; 32. LUCKEY ROBERTS; 33. MAXINE SULLIVAN; 34. JIMMY RUSHING; 35. JOE THOMAS; 36. SCOVILLE BROWNE; 37. STUFF SMITH; 38. BILL CRUMP; 39. COLEMAN HAWKINS; 40. RUDY POWELL; 41. OSCAR PETTIFORD; 42. SAHIB SHIHAB; 43. MARIAN McPARTLAND; 44. SONNY ROLLINS; 45. LAWRENCE BROWN; 46. MARY LOU WILLIAMS; 47. EMMETT BERRY; 48. THELONIOUS MONK; 49. VIC DICKENSON; 50. MILT HINTON; 51. LESTER YOUNG; 52. REX STEWART; 53. J. C. HEARD; 54. GERRY MULLIGAN; 55. ROY ELDRIDGE; 56. DIZZY GILLESPIE; 57. COUNT BASIE

(Top) Uptown Manhattan Ballroom Stomp variation. The symbolic gestures of purification are inseparable from the fertility ritual. Jive terms for blues-idiom communicants during the high times of the great ballroom bands of the thirties and forties: rug cutters, jitterbugs, Lindy hoppers. (Following page) The first, second, and third line in New York. The second line is seated on the curb with Count Basie. The third line consists of numbers 6, 14, 20, 21, 22, 23, 24, 43, and 54. (See key above).

no matter how much reviewers know about the classics of European music or any other music, they should presume to interpret and evaluate the work of blues musicians only when their familiarity with the special syntax of the blues convention is such that they are able to discern the relative emphasis each musician under consideration places on the definitive component of the idiom that is his actual frame of reference.

Not that the masterworks of the great European composers are not a fundamental part of all American musical sensibilities. Not that they are not also indispensable to the reporter's overall perception of context and universal significance. Nevertheless it is primarily in terms of his vernacular, which is to say, the actual working frame of reference, that a blues musician's sense of proportion must be judged.

Folk Art
and
Fine Art

So far as some people are concerned, to be sure, the only authentic blues music is that which is made up and performed by folk musicians. As such people see it, the elaborations, extensions, and refinements of the professional musicians are not the means by which the idiomatic is given the more inclusive range, greater precision of nuance, and more universal impact of fine art. What it all adds up to in their opinion is a basic violation of the priceless integrity of folk art.

Sometimes such people seem to have as many academic pieties about the inherent merits of folk music as some others seem to have about the intrinsic superiority of the music of the European recital hall. Few hesitate to declare, if only by implication, that folk art is the most valid, reliable, and comprehensive representation of actuality—as opposed to the distortions inherent in the artificialities of fine art. And yet in the case of blues music, it so happens that their own firsthand contact with the actualities of the experience being stylized is often extremely limited, to say the least. Nevertheless, they seem to regard themselves as being fully qualified somehow to reject the professional blues musician's preoccupation with craft and refinement out of hand. *Because in their view it can only result in pretension and decadence.*

But the assumption that folk expression is the unalloyed product of a direct stimulus/response interaction with natural environmental forces is fallacious. Folk expression is nothing if not conventional in the most fundamental sense of the word. Far from being spontaneous, as is so often supposed, it is formal. It is of its very nature traditional. The exact opposite of unadulterated invention growing out of the creative ingenuity of individuals uninhibited by regulations and unencumbered by the whims of fashion, it conforms to rigorously restrictive local, regional, which is to say provincial, ground rules that have been so completely established and accepted as to require little if any enforcement as such beyond initiation and apprenticeship instruction.

Perhaps what makes folk responses seem so natural and so free of ceremonial formality is the fact that they have long since become deeply ingrained habits! In any case the most distinctive feature of folk expression whether in the crafts or the arts is not its inherent orientation toward innovation but rather its all but total reliance on custom. The folk craftsman as artist is not primarily concerned with turning out something never before seen or heard of. He is concerned with doing what is expected of him, with showing how well he can do what he has been taught to do, with maintaining standards. Thus his subjects, themes, and his procedures are always those that are customary to his locality or province—even when the raw materials are not. Indeed he even clings to as many of the old ways as possible long after he has been transplanted to a new setting of radically different circumstances and requirements!

The seldom questioned assumption that folk creativity is the primal source or wellspring of sophisticated art and technology is also misleading. Being inherently conservative or traditional, folk expression is necessarily imitative and thus not primordial in any intrinsic sense at all but *derivative*. Moreover what it imitates and is itself derived from is such sophisticated art and technology as it has been able to come by through the process of corruption and vulgarization, or in a word, popularization. Folkways are always the old ways. Folklore is the old lore. Folk music is the old-time music. In other words, folk expression is old sophisticated technology, wisdom, and art, only now it is assumed to be indigenous to unsophisticated craftsmen, sages, and artists.

So actually it seems far more accurate to say that folk crafts, folk arts, and folklore are the source of much that in the natural process of things becomes the object of interest of sophisticated craftsmen and artists and in consequence is *reprocessed* or re-refined into sophisticated technology and art. Even as happens when some old hand-me-down folk ditty strikes the fancy of a sophisticated blues arranger/composer. Even as avant-garde artists appropriate a piece of commercial artwork that is a watered-down version of something copied from a sophisticated artist in the first place. The point, of course, is not the process of historical evolution of the dynamics of assimilation and feedback through which sophistication itself first came into being. What is at issue is whether folk expression is as pure a wellspring as it is so often taken for granted as being, and the evidence suggests only that it is one functional source among other functional sources—which include other sophisticated arts and crafts. After all, the creative process also involves counterstatement and extension.

Indeed, one very practical way to become properly oriented to the definitive characteristics of the work of any individual artist in any field is to approach it in terms of that which the artist is trying to counterstate as well as that which he is trying to extend. For the identity of each individual artist consists mainly of that unique combination of what he accepts among all the existing examples of stylization and is trying to extend, elaborate, and refine and maybe even transcend (as if to say: Yes, yes, yes, and also and also) on the one hand, and what he rejects as inadequate and misleading on the other and tries to counterstate with his own output (as if to say No, no, no; this is the way I see it, hear it, feel it).

Incidentally, sophisticated blues musicians extend, refine, and counterstate pop music, especially the thirty-two-bar show tune, in precisely the same manner as they do the traditional folk-type blues strain. Indeed, as the endless list of outstanding blues-idiom compositions derived from the songs of Jerome Kern, Irving Berlin, George Gershwin, Cole Porter, Harold Arlen, Vincent Youmans, and Walter Donaldson, among others, so clearly indicates, blues musicians proceed as if the Broadway musical were in fact a major source of relatively crude but fascinating folk materials!

●

As for those inclined to take exception to the notion that folk craftsmen and artists are lacking in imagination and inventiveness, perhaps they have forgotten what folk expression is really like. To begin with, it is predictable not experimental. In truth, it places no premium on newness as such. It is as far as is possible the

205

Tampa Red, *né* Hudson Whittaker, from Atlanta, Georgia, by way of Tampa, Florida, was a folk-oriented blues singer and guitar player who enjoyed something of a vogue in the late 1920s and early 1930s, mainly because of his various recordings of *It's Tight Like That*, which he wrote in collaboration with Thomas A. "Georgia Tom" Dorsey. Tampa Red and Georgia Tom are also remembered as accompanists on such Ma Rainey records as *Sleep Talking Blues*, *Tough Luck Blues*, *Daddy*, *Goodbye Blues*, *Sweet Rough Man*, *Black Eye Blues*, *Leaving This Morning*, and *Runaway Blues*, all of which are essentially traditional folksong blues ballads.

Charlie Christian, 1919–42, who attained world prominence during his two years (1939–41) as a sideman with Benny Goodman, the so-called King of Swing, was an instrumentalist who not only mastered all of the soulful nuances of traditional blues-idiom statement but also made of the guitar a hornlike solo vehicle with orchestral rank equivalent to the trumpet, the trombone, and the saxophone. Christian was born in Texas, grew up in the Oklahoma City of the Blue Devils and, like Lester Young and Charlie Parker, was a product of the territory dance circuit and Kansas City style after-hours jam sessions. His best-known records include *Solo Flight, Air Mail Special, Blues in B, Seven Come Eleven, A Smooth One,* and *Till Tom Special.*

same old stuff time and again. The same old-time tunes played (except for mistakes) the same old way, preferably on the same old instruments; the same old jokes and yarns and riddles and catches; the same old quilt patterns and needlework and pottery and straw baskets, and so on. Moreover those who do not adhere are far less likely to be applauded for being imaginative and inventive as derided for being ignorant and without talent and taste. It is the individual genius who deviates, experiments, and riffs. Folk craftsmen and artists conform. They do not accept the new until it has been well established. It is very obvious once you think about it: *Invention comes from people of special talent and genius, not from those who are circumscribed by routine.*

●

Nor should folk expression be confused with primitive, aboriginal, or savage arts and crafts. Folk arts and crafts are naïve. Primitive arts and crafts are sophisticated. They are not the crude imitation, corruption, vulgarization, or popularization of a more sophisticated stylization. They represent the very highest refinement of the rituals and technologies of a given culture. Also, no matter how relatively uncivilized or even utterly savage a given aboriginal culture may be, its art is the work of thoroughly trained professionals whose outlook being tribal-wide or kingdom-wide is anything but provincial in the sense that is characteristic of folk expression.

It may be that the only folk expression in many so-called primitive cultures exists at the level of children's play. The articles of carving and weaving for sale to tourists in contemporary African countries are of course another matter. They are not primitive; they are folk and pseudo-folk imitations of primitive carving and weaving. In any case it is also fallacious to assume that the origins of such Afro-American folkways, arts, and lore as may in fact have been derived directly from specific and clearly delineated African antecedents are folk origins.

There are also those who assume that folk simplicity represents a deliberate, down-to-earth, self-confident rejection of over-refinement and decadence. But once again the orthodox conformist is somehow made out to be a rebel. Once again the naïveté of the unsophisticated is represented as being a higher form of sophistication. It is no such thing. The truth is that folk artists are far more likely to be overimpressed and intimidated by fanciness

than repelled by it. Indeed nobody seems more vulnerable to pretentiousness, decadence, and even perversion. Who buys all the dime-store junk, all the tacky clothes and gaudy furniture? Who supports the pulp magazines, the grade-B movies, and the freak shows? Any two-bit city slicker knows that the homespun suckers head for the section of town where the clip joints are. Only the overenthusiastic partisans of folk art seem not to suspect that such ridicule as provincials heap on the highfalutin' is likely to come from uneasiness rather than any feeling of condescending superiority.

It is the nonfolk folk-art enthusiast, not the folk artist himself, who seems to dismiss most virtuosity as being tantamount to decadence and sterility. Folk artists almost always seem not only fascinated but overwhelmed by it—and only too eager to acquire and display as much of it as their limited technique will enable them to come by. Nor should it be forgotten that in the process many become top-level professionals who, when they look back, describe it all as a matter of personal improvement.

On the other hand all that is required for most professional blues musicians to play at the level of folk competence is less technical precision. Being for the most part a product of the very same folk experience as the folk artist they have always enjoyed comparable sensitivity to provincial nuances. In a sense all they have to do is relax into the proper fuzziness of articulation. Certainly it is not a matter of the folk artist being less artificial. It is all a matter of stylization. Perhaps the folk artist seems less artificial, but the fact is that he simply sticks to the old familiar modes of stylization, and the result is that customary artificiality which is taken for granted as the natural way, but which is no less artificial withal. The stylizations of Leadbelly, Blind Lemon Jefferson, Tampa Red, Leroy Carr, Lonnie Johnson, Muddy Waters, and Lightnin' Hopkins are not less artificial than those of, say, Floyd Smith, Charlie Christian, Otis Spann, and George Benson, only less sophisticated.

Still, many of the partisans of folk expression who also admire Bessie Smith, for instance, seem to do so not because they esteem her as the great professional that she was (whose stylistic innovations represent the very highest level of idiomatic refinement) but rather because they regard her as a natural phenomenon with a

Leadbelly, famed as a master of the twelve-string guitar, was an outstanding representative of traditional folk-blues statement. His early work is that of an authentic downhome provincial. His later performances were mostly pseudofolk presentations for audiences that were more curious than involved.

Bessie Smith transformed traditional folk-blues ballads into fine art of universal impact and significance. The value of a work of art, as André Malraux once said, "depends neither upon its emotion nor its detachment but upon the blending of its content with the method of its expression." Such a blending also enabled her to make fine art out of run-of-the-mill show biz pop and novelty tunes like *Gimme A Pigfoot* and *Cake Walking Babies*.

deeply stirring voice that was a great vehicle of honest expression precisely because it struck them as being untrained and hence unstylized. Perhaps they assume that her music is necessarily as crude as her diction so often was. It is not. Moreover, far from restricting herself to the limitations of her diction, she almost always worked with the most sophisticated professionals available in the idiom. Such accompanists as Clarence Williams, Fletcher Henderson, James P. Johnson, Porter Grainger, Louis Armstrong, Joe Smith, Buster Bailey, Don Redman, and Coleman Hawkins could hardly be considered folk musicians by any standard.

But after all what really seems to underlie most of the notions of those who prefer folk art to fine art are the same old essentially sentimental assumptions that make for pastoral literature (and for political theories about noble savages). Thus, much the same as pastoral poetry presents its rustics as being on better terms with life than courtiers because they are closer to nature, so would promoters of folk art as the true art have you believe that a provincial musical sensibility is somehow a greater endowment than a more cosmopolitan sensibility plus a greater mastery of technique. It absolutely is not. It limits not only what folk artists can do but also what they can perceive and imagine in the first place.

On the other hand, all too often the professional blues musician's involvement with elaboration, extension, and refinement does indeed get out of control and degenerate into pretentious display and a mindless pursuit of novelty for its own sake—or in the name of some sophomoric conception of progress. In fact, those who shift their primary orientation from the ballroom to the concert hall (giving up the immediate response of the dancers for that of the reviewer!) seem especially vulnerable to such decadence and pretentiousness.

No less pretentious, however, are those pseudo-folk blues musicians whose experiences are no longer those that gave rise to the traditional folk-blues folk song, but who limit themselves to traditional folk modes even as they address themselves to the problems of the New York Stock Exchange, the proper way to conduct international relations, space technology, and the like, for the edification of chic patrons of avant-garde night clubs, sometimes while performing on electronic instruments that are nothing if not as *dernier cri* as the limousines and jetliners they travel around in

Duke Ellington in 1928. That Ellington's music represents refinement, elaboration, and extension of folk art into fine art is obvious enough, but as is entirely consistent with the function of fine art in the first place, the Ellington influence has in turn also been noticeable among folk musicians both sacred and secular. Indeed when he began using conventional church singers in his sacred concerts he was working with musical sensibilities that had long since been so deeply influenced by his dance music that hardly any adjustment of modes was necessary.

for the most part.

There is much to be said for such blues music as is indeed folk song. But however much there is to say about the authentic earthiness of Blind Lemon Jefferson and Leadbelly, for instance, without whose best output no collection of twentieth-century American music should be considered truly representative, there is a good deal more to be said for the no less authentic extensions and refinements that have resulted from the playful options taken by such consecrated professionals as Jelly Roll Morton, Louis Armstrong, Bessie Smith, Lester Young, Charlie Parker, and Duke Ellington. Because the point is that unless the idiom is not only robust and earthy enough but also refined enough with a range comprehensive enough to reflect the subtleties and complexities of contemporary experience, it is not likely to be a very effective counteragent of the blues or any other demons, devils, or dragons.

The preeminent embodiment of the blues musician as artist was Duke Ellington, who, in the course of fulfilling the role of entertainer, not only came to address himself to the basic imperatives of music as a fine art but also achieved the most comprehensive sythesis, extension, and refinement to date of all the elements of blues musicianship. Indeed so all-inclusive was Ellington's synthesis that it amounts to a special vocabulary and syntax of orchestration.

But then as Ernest Hemingway wrote in *Death in the Afternoon* about bull fighting, regarding it not as a folk spectacle but a fine art practiced by individuals who were by exclusive devotion and training the most sophisticated professionals:

> All art is only done by the individual. The individual is all you ever have and all schools only serve to classify their members as failures. *The individual, the great artist when he comes, uses everything that has been discovered or known about his art up to that point, being able to accept or reject in a time so short it seems that the knowledge was born with him, rather than that he takes instantly what it takes the ordinary man a lifetime to know, and then the great artist goes beyond what has been done or known and makes something of his own.*

214

(Top) The Duke Ellington Orchestra of 1926. (Left to right) Ellington; Tricky Sam Nanton, trombone; Sonny Green, drums; Bubber Miley, trumpet; Harry Carney, baritone, clarinet, bass clarinet; Wellman Braud, tuba, bass fiddle; Rudy Jackson, reeds; Freddie Guy, banjo; Nelson Kincaid, reeds; and Ellsworth Reynolds, guitar, violin. At this time the evolution of the great Ellington orchestral vehicle was definitely underway. The highly distinctive voicings of Miley, Nanton, and Carney were to become indispensable elements of the Ellington sound. (Bottom) Johnny Hodges, alto, and Barney Bigard, clarinet and tenor, two other fundamental elements of the Ellington sound, were added early in 1928. The Ellington orchestra of the early 1930s enjoyed international renown because of recordings of such Ellington compositions as *East St. Louis Toodle-oo, Mood Indigo, The Mooche, Black and Tan Fantasy, Birmingham Breakdown,* and *Rockin' in Rhythm.*

(Top) Duke Ellington directing from the keyboard. (Bottom) Ellington and his orchestra of 1942. (Left to right) Otto Hardwick, alto; Juan Tizol, trombone; Shorty Baker, trumpet; Ray Nance, trumpet, violin, vocals; Harry Carney, baritone, alto, clarinet, bass clarinet; Betty Roché, vocals; Rex Stewart, cornet; Johnny Hodges, alto; Ben Webster, tenor; Chauncey Haughton, reeds; Tricky Sam Nanton, trombone; Wallace Jones, trumpet; Lawrence Brown, trombone; and Sonny Greer, drums. The guitar at Ellington's right was played by Freddie Guy. The bass fiddle in front of Hardwick was played by Junior Raglan, the replacement for Jimmy Blanton (inset) who, during his tenure with Ellington from 1939 to his death in 1941 at age thirty, established the string bass as a major solo voice among other blues instruments.

216

Ellington (left) and Billy Strayhorn (right), 1915–67, who was Ellington's own chief arranger and collaborator from 1939 until 1967. Strayhorn, whose first work as apprentice arranger was *I'm Checkin' Out Goombye*, was the composer of *Take the A Train*, which supplanted *East St. Louis Toodle-oo* as Ellington's theme, as well as *Johnny Come Lately, Raincheck, Passion Flower, Day Dream, Midriff,* and *Boodah*. He also collaborated on several Ellington suites, including *Such Sweet Thunder, Suite Thursday,* and *The Perfume Suite*.

VICTOR

"HIS MASTER'S VOICE"
REG. U. S. PAT. OFF.   MARCAS REGISTRADAS

For best results
use Victor Needles

27380-A

TAKE THE "A" TRAIN—Fox Trot
(*Tome el Tren "A"*)
(Billy Strayhorn)
Duke Ellington and his
Famous Orchestra

217

The Ellington orchestra of the late 1930s. (Back row, left to right) Sonny Greer, drums; Arthur Whetsol, trumpet; Juan Tizol, trombone; Hayes Alvis, bass; Billy Taylor, bass; Freddie Guy, guitar; Harry Carney, baritone, alto, clarinet, bass clarinet; Lawrence Brown, trombone; Otto Hardwick, alto. (Front row, left to right) Ellington; Johnny Hodges, alto; Barney Bigard, clarinet, tenor; Cootie Williams, trumpet; Tricky Sam Nanton, trombone; Rex Stewart, cornet. With the exception of replacements for Whetsol and several shifts in bass players, this is the great lineup heard on *Tootin' Through the Roof, Old King Dooji, Serenade to Sweden, Boy Meets Horn, Slap Happy, The Gal from Joe's, Diminuendo in Blue, Crescendo in Blue, Portrait of the Lion, Ridin' on a Blue Note,* and *I Let a Song Go Out of My Heart.*

221

Five outstanding arrangers and composers. (Top, left) Benny Carter, whose work is better known by fellow musicians than by the general public, is especially noted for his scoring for reeds. (Top, right) Sy Oliver established his reputation with the Jimmie Lunceford orchestra, for which he constructed *Dream of You, Four or Five Times, My Blue Heaven, For Dancers Only, Cheatin' on Me, Ain't She Sweet*, and numerous others. (Bottom, left) Eddie Durham, whose arrangements for the Blue Devils, the Bennie Moten orchestra, and Count Basie played a crucial part in making the Kansas City emphasis a fundamental element of blues-idiom musicianship. He composed or collaborated on the composition of *Moten Swing, Topsy, Time Out, Lafayette, Out the Window*, and *Good Morning Blues*. (Bottom, right) Budd Johnson was responsible for such items in the classic Earl Hines repertoire as *Piano Man, Riff Medley, XYZ, Number 19*, and *Grand Terrace Shuffle*.

Don Redman, 1900–64, who prepared written scores for the original Fletcher Henderson big band (1923–26), is generally credited with being the first important arranger/composer of dance-band orchestrations. In point of fact, Redman was constructing scores for the Broadway Syncopators, a band from Pittsburgh, as early as 1922. His best-known compositions are *The Chant of the Weed, Cherry, Save it Pretty Mama,* and *Gee Baby, Ain't I Good to You?* Arrangements he did for Henderson include *The Dicty Blues, Copenhagen, T.N.T., Shanghai Shuffle, Alabamy Bound, Sugarfoot Stomp, The Stampede, Hop Off,* and *Jackass Blues.* Among those for McKinney's Cotton Pickers, for whom he left Henderson, are *Miss Hannah, Peggy,* and *That's the Way I Feel Today.*

Those who regard Ellington as the most representative American composer have good reason. Not unlike Emerson, Melville, Whitman, Twain, Hemingway, and Faulkner in literature, he quite obviously has converted more of the actual texture and vitality of American life into first-rate universally appealing music than anybody else. Moreover he has done so in terms of such vernacular devices of blues musicianship as vamps, riffs, breaks, fills, call-and-response sequences, idiomatic syncopation, downhome folk timbres, drum-oriented horns, strings, and so on. By comparison the sonorities, not to mention the devices of Charles Ives, Walter Piston, Virgil Thomson, Aaron Copland, Roger Sessions, John Cage, and Elliott Carter, for example, seem if not downright European, at least as European as American. In any case the Ellington canon, which consists mainly of three-minute dance pieces, is by far the most comprehensive orchestration of the actual sound and beat of life in the United States ever accomplished by a single composer. *Mainstem, Harlem Airshaft, Echoes of Harlem, Across the Track Blues, Sepia Panorama,* and *Showboat Shuffle* are only a random few of an endless flow of matchless evocations of the spirit of place in America. Nor is any other American composer responsible for instrumental extensions of American voice and speech that are more significant those that are so immediately manifest in *Mood Indigo, Harmony in Harlem, In a Jam, Ko-Ko, Concerto for Cootie,* and *Rockabye River.* Even when Ellington addresses himself to natural phenomenon, as in *Lightnin'* and *Dusk,* or to such universal rituals as the chase, as in *Cotton Tail,* or is just playing with instrumental possibilities, as in *Boy Meets Horn* and *Riding on a Blue Note,* his voice and accent are uniquely American.

The Blues
as Statement

Ordinarily blues musicians do not show very much conscious involvement with the philosophical implications of what they play. Most often their primary musical concerns seem to be those of the artisan. Accordingly, what they almost always seem to give most of their attention to are the practical details of the specific convention of stylization in terms of which they perform. Thus shoptalk as well as arguments about such professional matters as the characteristics and peculiarities of musical instruments and accessories, fundamentals of and innovations in technique, the merits and shortcomings of various systems of execution and exercise manuals, keynote preferences, the eccentricities of arrangers and the idiosyncrasies of other musicians, especially those they admire, are quite commonplace among them. But beyond that it is mostly as if they expect the music to speak for itself.

Those who respond to questions (seldom asked by other musicians) about their involvement with some currently fashionable, though not necessarily popular, stylistic movement, do so for the most part only with vague, superficial, hand-me-down generalities about progress, changing with the times, giving the public something new, making a new contribution, or about finding themselves. Even when some of those who aligned themselves with bop, cool, and the special extensions of John Coltrane and Ornette Coleman, for example, used to claim that the new music represented a new and even revolutionary message, they never really addressed themselves to the content of the new message, or the old one either for that matter. Indeed what they say about the signifi-

(Top) Ornette Coleman, one of the most spectacular of the post-Charlie Parker musicians. Some of his most enthusiastic supporters regard his innovations as representing a radical break with all tradition and others hear in them a return to the deepest roots of the blues idiom; but as of 1976, such vintage Coleman compositions as *Lonely Woman, Congeniality, Peace, Blues Connotation. Free Jazz, Harlem's Manhattan,* and *Skies of America* seem to be better known and better received by concert-goers and patrons of "new thing" night clubs than by traditional dance-hall, honky-tonk, night-club, and holiday revelers. (Bottom, left) Thelonious Monk, whose status as innovator is comparable to that of Christian, Gillespie, and Parker, is in a sense also a very special descendent of the old downhome honky-tonk piano player who likes to sit alone in the empty ballroom and play around with unconventional chord combinations and rhythms for his own private enjoyment. There is something of the empty ballroom *étude* in almost all of Monk's compositions, which include *Epistrophy, 'Round About Midnight, Straight No Chaser, Brilliant Corners, Let's Call This, Nutty, Work, and Misterioso.* (Bottom, right) Miles Davis, who achieved prominence as a sideman with Charlie Parker and later became the touchstone of the so-called Cool Movement, is perhaps the most influential trumpet player since the bop decade.

John Coltrane, who received his first wide recognition as a so-called Hard Bop tenor player in Miles Davis's combo of the 1950s and who, along with Ornette Coleman, became one of the most important innovators of the 1960s, is essentially a post-Charlie Parker instrumental extension of the traditional hard-driving blues shouter. Such Coltrane compositions as *Blue Train, Locomotion*, and *Traneing In* also represent post-bop avant-garde elaborations and refinements of traditional blues-idiom railroad onomatopoeia.

229

cance of Charlie Parker, Dizzy Gillespie, Miles Davis, and John Coltrane, among others, including Thelonious Monk, Ornette Coleman, and John Lewis, almost always suggests that they are either far more interested in the social, economic, and political status of the blues musician than in his fundamental function, or that they may confuse the two.

In any case, not very many blues musicians seem to bother themselves very much about the fundamental personal and social function of percussive incantation, purification and fertility rituals, and ceremonies of affirmation. But such rituals and ceremonies are precisely what their work is very much about even so. Not only do most perform in special ceremonial costumes of one sort or another to begin with, for example, and not only are the bandstand procedures and manners of honky-tonk piano players, street-corner harmonica and guitar players, night-club and vaudeville entertainers, members of cocktail-lounge combos and dance-band sidemen alike always likely to be as ceremonial as functional; but so more often than not are their attire and deportment in most other situations.

Indeed, the off-duty blues musician tends to remain in character much as does the Minister of the Gospel, and as he makes the rounds he also receives a special deference from the Saturday Night Revelers equivalent to that given off-duty ministers by Sunday Morning Worshipers. The ever-so-casual speech, dress, and movements of Lester Young, for instance, having a sip and a chat with friends or fans in a gin mill in the middle of a midweek afternoon were no less stylized and ceremonial than the traditional formalities of the rhetoric, vestments, and bearing of a member of any priesthood. Nor are the most casual-seeming recording-studio procedures any less a matter of ritual. Most of the slouching about, the jive talk, the joking, and even the nonchalance is as deliberately stylized as is most of the stage business on the bandstand during a performance for a regular audience.

Nor are any of the blues musician's role-defining mannerisms, whether on- or off-stage, likely to be lost on the apprentices. An outstanding case in point is Louis Armstrong, Promethean Culture Hero that he was. In spite of all the uneasiness that some of the minstrel-show aspects of his stage routine caused among socially conscious U.S. Negroes, the extent of his influence on the speech,

Lester Young wearing the black, very low, crushed porkpie hat that became his sartorial trade-mark. Off the bandstand he was almost always the coolly hip but approachable and considerate loner. His quietly jocular speech was full of such jive terms as *eyes, big eyes, nice eyes,* or *bells* or *cool* or *ding dong* to express approval; *getting bruised* for failing; *getting straight* or *getting with it* for succeeding; *buzzing* or *whispering* for backbiting, and so on.

(Top) Lester and porkpie splitting. (Bottom) Lester resplendent in chalk stripes, backstage with a group of admirers. Notable among them is Lionel Hampton, the great jump-band leader, who is imitating the notorious forty-five-degree angle that was Young's main concession to bandstand showmanship.

Louis Armstrong, the fashion plate. At one time his regular wardrobe is reported to have contained as many as seventy-five suits, not to mention a similar abundance of shoes, shirts, and ties. Armstrong not only used to enjoy going out on the town but also had a reputation for being one of the very best ballroom dancers among the musicians of his time.

DECCA

Fox Trot
Vocal Chorus by
Louis Armstrong

GOT A BRAN' NEW SUIT
From Messrs. Shubert Presentation
"At Home Abroad"
(ARTHUR SCHWARTZ-HOWARD DIETZ)
LOUIS ARMSTRONG and his
ORCHESTRA
579 B

234

(Opposite page) Duke Ellington, who sometimes liked to refer to himself as a "pedestrian minstrel, a primitive pedestrian minstrel," posing as a street musician in aristocratic plaids and against the background of a Cotton Club mural. (Above) A portrait of the artist as the composer with all the prerequisite personal experience and cosmopolitan *savoir faire* that went into the making of *Sophisticated Lady*.

Freddy Keppard and Sidney Bechet in Chicago, circa 1918, wearing single- and double-breasted versions of the dapper threads of the period. Keppard, who had left New Orleans in 1911, was then the hottest trumpet player in town. Bechet, as a member of Will Marion Cook's Southern Syncopated Orchestra of 1919, was the first performer to inspire European critics to regard blues music as art rather than as a form of light entertainment.

Miles Davis, whose influence as innovator in the 1950s was somewhat comparable to that of Armstrong in the 20s and 30s, rejected the image Armstrong projected as vaudeville entertainer, but continued the Armstrong tradition as pacesetter for men's fashions. In 1959 Davis was voted one of the ten best dressed men in America.

professional mannerisms, and grooming of blues musicians everywhere is comparable to that which he has had on their instrumental and vocal technique. Much of the ritual jive talk and many of the ceremonial gestures used by most sophisticated blues musicians (and dandyish hangers-on, also known as hipsters) are derived directly from Armstrong during his heyday back in the late twenties and the thirties. It was Armstrong who started musicians referring to themselves as cats and to their control and stamina as their chops (originally the brass player's lips), and to playing well as getting away (and hence, being gone!). It was also Louis Armstrong who popularized such ritualized greetings as What you say, Gates; Well, what you know, Jim; Well, lay it on me, Cousin, Hoss, Home, etc.; Well, give me some skin, man, and endless riffs thereon, with which sophisticated blues musicians still salute each other (sometimes also along with a mumbo-jumbo handshaking, palm-slapping, or finger-touching routine) precisely as if they belong to the same very special fraternal order, which of course they do.

At one point in a series of interviews with one Tom Davin, published in *The Jazz Review* in 1959 and 1960, James P. Johnson, one of the most formidable of the Harlem Stride piano players, goes to some lengths to show how fundamental to the blues musician's apprenticeship as a performer was what in effect was a consciousness of his ritual status and his skill at role playing. He begins by telling about how when Willie (The Lion) Smith, who was a sharp dresser and a fine dancer as well as one of the most fearsome piano players in town, walked into a place, his every move was a picture. Johnson in response to a question then goes on to say, "Yes, every move we made was studied, practiced, and developed just like it was a complicated piano piece." Then he not only describes a typical entrance routine but goes into the most minute detail about costuming, including material, the cut, shoes, hats, jewelry, prices, tailors, and hair preparations.

When he was a young fellow, he continues, he was

> very much impressed with such manners. . . . You had to have an attitude, a style of behaving that was your personal, professional trade-mark. . . . The older Clef Club musicians were artists at this kind of acting. The club was the place to go study these glamorous characters. I got a lot of my style from ticklers like Floyd Keppard, who I knew in Jersey City, Dan Avery, Bob Hawkins, Lester Wil-

JELLY ROLL" MORTON
Originator of Jazz & Stomps
And his
RED HOT PEPPERS

Jelly Roll Morton in the wine red jacket with tie to match, white slacks, and two-toned shoes he used to wear while conducting. He is said to have owned as many as a hundred and fifty suits back in the late 1920s and early 1930s. He also used to wear a diamond ring, a diamond horseshoe tie pin, a watch circled with diamonds, a diamond-studded gold belt buckle, and a huge half-carat diamond in one of his front teeth.

VE
"HIS MASTER'S VOICE"
VICTOR
Orthophonic
Recording   20415-A
DOCTOR JAZZ–STOMP
(Joe Oliver)
Jelly-Roll Morton's Red Hot Peppers
Vocal refrain by Jelly-Roll Morton
VICTOR TALKING MACHINE CO.
Camden, N.J.
VE

240

Opposite page: (Bottom, left) Harry "Sweets" Edison, trumpet, and Illinois Jacquet, tenor sax, sidemen in the Count Basie orchestra, in an informal session in the 1940s. (Bottom, right) Duke Ellington about town in 1940. (Above, top) Dizzy Gillespie and orchestra in standard casual attire for a studio session in 1947. (Bottom) Count Basie and sidemen in come-as-you-are for rehearsal and studio. (Left to right) Jo Jones wearing high-waist drape that won the approval of hipsters across the nation, Count Basie in one of his usual muted but well-tailored theater-district business suits, Walter Page in the vest and pants of a conservatively cut three-piece street outfit, and Buck Clayton in an elegant candy-stripe, tab-collar shirt and tie.

(Left) Dizzy Gillespie, who was dizzy like a fox. Many of his followers vehemently condemned the role of blues musician as entertainer and dance-hall performer and sought what they seemed to regard as the greater dignity of the staid artist of the recital stage. Gillespie, however, was no less a vaudeville-type showman than Armstrong before him, and was forever "putting the audience on" with sly digs and mischievous pranks. The most authentic source of bop fashions at the height of his popularity in the 1940s, he seems to have regarded clothes mainly as stage costume. (Right, top and bottom) Charlie Parker is not noted for having had any of the typical blues musician's usual involvement with high fashion. His clothes were never out of fashion, to be sure, but on stage with Gillespie and Davis (opposite page, top and bottom) he sometimes looked baggy in the breeches.

243

son, Freddie Tunstall, Kid Sneeze, Abba Labba, Willie Smith, and many others. . . .

I've seen Jelly Roll Morton, who had a great attitude, approach a piano. He would take his overcoat off. It had a special lining that would catch everybody's eye. So he would turn it inside out and, instead of folding it, he would lay it lengthwise along the top of the upright piano. He would do this very slowly, very carefully, and very solemnly as if that coat was worth a fortune and had to be handled very tenderly.

Then he'd take a big silk handkerchief, shake it out to show it off properly, and dust off the stool. He'd sit down then, hit his special chord (every tickler had his special chord, like a signal), and he'd be gone!

Every tickler kept these attitudes even when he was socializing at parties or just visiting. They were his professional personality and prepared the audience for the artistic performance to come.

Not all blues musicians place such obvious emphasis on costume and role playing, needless to say. Some proceed for the most part as if they regard music as simply another means of earning a living much the same as any other means of livelihood, and some give the impression that they play mainly because it happens to be the thing for which they have the best technical qualifications. And yet even so, not only do they dress, act, and talk more like other blues musicians than like anybody else, but some of their most casual references to the most routine matters of performance are likely to reflect a functional awareness of their involvement with ritual and role fulfillment:

"Man, if they ain't patting their feet, you ain't swinging and ain't nothing happening, because they spending their money to have a good time, and that's your job. . . .

"People look at you sitting up there and they kinda expect you to be dressed kinda special, you know what I mean? You don't have to overdo it with all that old jive-time monkey stuff. You know what I mean. I'm talking about they come in somewhere they might try to tear the joint up before it's over but they still like to come in there and see some kind of special decorations and all that, because it might be the same old thing every night to you but you got to remember it's always a special occasion with them. That's why most bands wear uniforms. Like baseball teams. Because a baseball game is a special event. And when a band has its own uniform it also looks more professional.

"You know how old Count used to come on like Gang Busters, with the rhythm already up here and the brass up there and the reeds solid in there. And then he might let the alto or one of the trumpets do a quick get-away and then tickle things up himself on the piano and then sic them two bad assed tenors, old Hershel and old Lester on you and goddamn! Sometimes we do that too. That's how we used to hit when the man wanted to get the house warmed up and cutting from the gitgo. Sometimes we might do a whole set like that, and then a set to settle them down, and then we might bring on a girl or maybe a guy or maybe both and do some pop ballads, some sweet and some on some real snappy arrangements with the band jiving and signifying and shouting and carrying on in the background. Then after a while we always bring on the main blues singer, like when old Count used to call Jimmy Rushing. Old Duke's main blues singer was always old Johnny Hodges on that alto, even when he had Herb Jeffries. From then on we got them grooving until wrap-up time, when we ride on out like till we meet again."

On the other hand there are also those who place primary emphasis on costumes and stage business. Back during the time when the so-called bop and so-called cool movements were being publicized as the living (which is to say ultimate) end of all blues stylization and hence the only possible route to true hipness or in-ness, some used to dress the part of being appropriately *modern* and *progressive* by wearing a beret and heavy-frame glasses like Dizzy Gillespie, the then current pacesetter on trumpet. Many, perhaps many more, used to act the part by aping the self-centered bandstand mannerisms of Charlie Parker, the veritable touchstone of the movement, who seems to have struck them as being so totally wrapped up in the esoteric ramifications of what he was expressing with such overwhelming elegance that nothing else

●

(Following page) (Left to right) Don Byas, tenor; Buck Clayton, trumpet; Red Allen, trumpet; Specs Powell, drums; Count Basie, piano; J. C. Higginbotham, trombone; Ken Kersey; Pete Johnson, piano; and Lena Horne, vocalist, during a jam session in New York in 1938. Over the years jazz critics have placed primary emphasis on the informality of the jam session—pointing out quite accurately that it is based on improvisations rather than written scores and has no set program or repertoire. Frequently only one or two selections will be performed during the course of an entire all-night session. There is never any set instrumentation. Usually there is a rhythm section of some kind (often with less than the full conventional complement of piano, drums, bass fiddle, and guitar or banjo on hand), with almost any combination of instrumental voices (sometimes so numerous that they have to play in shifts). But even as critics have represented jam sessions as informal musical contests, they have somehow left the impression that they permit more freedom than is actually the case. A jam session, for all its casual atmosphere, is not a wide open free-for-all where anything goes. *It is the exclusive province of the dedicated professional, to whom blues music is nothing if not a fine art requiring the very highest level of technical mastery of one's instrument as well as unflagging spur-of-the-moment inventiveness.* In order to acquit himself with competence in a jam session, a blues musician must not only be a virtuoso performer but must also be able to create in a split second (and in response to and in the presence of peers) the most complex figures and runs. Elegance under pressure or bust.

245

To My Pal Lee

NG'S SECRET "9" BALL TEAM
NEW ORLEANS, LA.
1931

in the world mattered anymore, not even the paying customers.

Which of course was not the case at all with Parker himself, who, true to his Kansas City upbringing, was, with all his individuality and in spite of all his personal problems, nothing if not a sensational crowd pleaser. Nevertheless such was the primacy of role playing among some of his self-styled followers that sometimes it was as if the only audience beyond themselves that counted was other musicians, whom they were not nearly so interested in entertaining as impressing and being one-up on. Not that they really wanted to be left alone. No blues-idiom musicians were ever so recital oriented. They wanted audiences that would give them their undivided attention, not dancers out to have their own good time.

But thus did they become involved in another ritual altogether. For the ceremony they are concerned with is not a matter of dance-beat-oriented incantation leading to celebration. They proceed as if playing music were a sacred act of self-expression that can only be defiled by such Dionysian revelry as characterizes the Saturday Night Function, and thus should be restricted to Amen Corner witnesses, and to journalists who (despite their own incurable squareness) will give it maximum publicity in the national and international media and thus reemphasize its exclusiveness and gain new converts at the same time.

What it all represents is an attitude toward the nature of human experience (and the alternatives of human adjustment) that is both elemental and comprehensive. It is a statement about confronting

•

(Preceding spread) The enthusiasm for baseball that has long been so widespread among blues musicians is remarkably in character with their involvement in rituals of elegant endeavor and perseverance in unfavorable circumstances. The overall attitude toward the nature of things that is implicit in a baseball game is not at all unlike the pragmatism that underlies the blues statement: Not only are there bad times as well as good times, but even during the best of seasons when your team wins more games than its opponents, most of its efforts end in failure. The very best batters are not only hard put to hit safely on an average of three out of ten times but miss the ball more often than they hit it whenever they swing the bat. Most base runners do not score. The very best pitchers not only give up bases on balls and have their best pitches end up as hits and even as home runs, but also get knocked out of the box from time to time. And yet the competing players and partisan spectators alike accept such adversity as a part of the game, which otherwise would not last the customary nine innings. In fact, the whole point of sportsmanship is to condition people to win without arrogance and to fail with grace. As deeply disappointed as a team and its rooters are when its most dependable hitter strikes out in the ninth inning with tying and winning runs on third and second base, everybody would be scandalized if he then became so embarrassed that he ran off and spent the rest of the day crying and cursing himself. What is expected is that he realize that for all his great skill, past record, and heroic effort, you cannot win them all.

the complexities inherent in the human situation and about improvising or experimenting or riffing or otherwise playing with (or even gambling with) such possibilities as are also inherent in the obstacles, the disjunctures, and the jeopardy. It is also a statement about perseverance and about resilience and thus also about the maintenance of equilibrium despite precarious circumstances and about achieving elegance in the very process of coping with the rudiments of subsistence.

It is thus the musical equivalent of the epic, which Kenneth Burke in *Attitudes toward History* categorizes as a Frame of Acceptance as opposed to a Frame of Rejection. Burke is discussing poetic statements in terms of whether they represent a disposition to accept the universe with all its problems or to protest against it, and in the category of Acceptance he also includes tragedy, comedy, humor, and the ode. What is accepted, of course, is not the status quo nor any notion of being without potentiality nor even the spirit of the time; what is accepted is the all too obvious fact that human existence is almost always a matter of endeavor and hence also a matter of heroic action.

In the category of Rejection, which he characterizes as representing a negative emphasis while also pointing out that the differentiation cannot be absolute, Burke places the plaint or elegy, satire, burlesque (plus such related forms as polemic and caricature), the grotesque (which he says "focuses in mysticism"), and the didactic, which today is usually called propaganda. At bottom, what is rejected by such statements of lamentation, protestation, and exaggeration is the very existence of the circumstances that make heroic endeavor necessary. Not that most of the lamentation and protestation may not be in interest of better times, but what is featured all the same almost always turns out to be the despicable, the forlorn, the dissipated, and the down and out.

The trouble, however, is that when you get down to details rituals of self-expression are beyond criticism. Anything goes because it is all a matter of the innermost truth of the performer's being. Thus if his musicianship seems lacking in any way, it is not because he is working in an idiom with which the listener is unfamiliar but which has a different set of requirements, but rather because it is the best of all possible ways to express what the musician in question is all about! The self-portrait (and/or the

251

personal signature) that emerges from the music of Jelly Roll Morton, King Oliver, Bessie Smith, Louis Armstrong, Duke Ellington, Lester Young, and Charlie Parker is not primarily a matter of such egotistical self-documentation but rather of the distinction with which they fulfilled inherited roles in the traditional ritual of blues confrontation and purgation, and of life affirmation and continuity through improvisation. Incidentally, the revolutionary nature of their innovations and syntheses was not nearly so much a matter of a quest for newness for the sake of change as of the modifications necessary in order to maintain the definitive essentials of the idiom.

In one sense Charlie Parker's widely imitated innovations did indeed represent a radical counterstatement of certain aspects of the blues convention that had been so overworked that he had come to regard them as the same old thing. But for all that, Parker, unlike so many of his so-called progressive but often only pretentious followers, was not looking for ways to stop blues from swinging; he was looking for ways to make it swing even more, and sometimes when he really got going he achieved an effect that was both flippantly humorous and soulfully lyrical at the same time. On balance, Parker, it is true, must be considered as having been more of a jam-session musician than a dance-hall musician as such; but for him the jam session was not primarily an experimental workshop; it was to remain essentially the same old multidimensional good-time after-hours gathering it had always been. The experimental innovations were mainly a matter of having something special to strut your stuff with when your turn came to solo on the riff-solo-riff merry-go-round.

Nor should the overall personal and social implications of the blues statement be confused with the flamboyant costumes and overstylized mannerisms of the so-called hipsters (erstwhile hip cats and hep cats), the dandies, fops, and swells of the idiom. After all, the hipster's behavior is the same as that of the dilettante, who lives the "literary life" but only dabbles in literature as such. He knows all the right names, and like the *flaneur* of the art galleries he is also nothing if not up to date on what is in vogue as of tomorrow. In a sense he is also like the sedentary spectator whose concerns are completely circumscribed by the world of his favorite sport. Costuming himself and sounding off as if he *belongs* are

Nothing is more down-to-earth or more obvious than the ever-steady but somehow also ever-flexible Kansas City Four/Four dance beat. Nor is anything more subtle or less monotonous. Jo Jones, the most masterful, influential, and enduring of Kansas City percussionists, is as widely celebrated for the way he signifies with his sticks and wire brushes as for the way he testifies, bears witness, exhorts, annotates, approves, or otherwise comments—not only with his sticks and his foot pedals but also with his mallets and sometimes with his bare hands. Moreover, musicians and dancers alike almost always seem to respond as readily to his most offhand insinuations as to his most forthright declarations and most authoritative decrees.

about the extent of his involvement.

In any case the hipster's application of the disposition to riff with elegance is usually limited to jiving and woofing on his street-corner hangout and to shucking and stuffing along the mainstem, as if the night club, the ballroom, the music hall, and the bars that the performers, gamblers, and the sporting crowd frequent were what life itself were all about. Indeed some hipsters, not unlike some churchgoers, are so preoccupied with the trappings and procedures of the ceremonial occasion per se that their involvement amounts to idolatry. They misconstrue the symbol and the ritual reenactment as the thing itself.

There are those who regard blues music as a statement of rejection because to them it represents the very opposite of heroism. To many it represents only the anguished outcry of the victim, displaying his or her wounds and saying that it is all a lowdown dirty shame. To some, such purification as is involved is not of the atmosphere (which is indeed a matter of epic heroism) but of the individual, whose action is an effort not to contend but to "let it all hang out"; which, however, removes blues music from the realm of ritual and art and makes it a form of psychological therapy (although there is a literary analogy even so: the tear-jerker, the penny dreadful, the pulp confession story, which is almost always the sad saga of a victim). But thus also is blues music mistaken for that of the torch singer.

Blues music, however, is neither negative nor sentimental. It counterstates the torch singer's sob story, sometimes as if with the snap of two fingers! What the customary blues-idiom dance movement reflects is a disposition to encounter obstacle after obstacle as a matter of course. Such jive expressions as *getting with it* and *taking care of business* are references to heroic action. Indeed the improvisation on the break, which is required of blues-idiom musicians and dancers alike, is precisely what epic heroism is based on. In all events, such blues-idiom dance gesture is in effect an exercise in heroic action, and each selection on a dance program is, in a sense, a rehearsal for another of a never-ending sequence of escapades *as is suggested by the very fact that each not so much begins and ends as continues: And one and two and three and four and another one and a two and a three and a four and also and also and also* from vamp to outchorus to the next vamp.

Epilogue

The main thing that it is always about is the also and also of dragging, driving, jumping, kicking, swinging, or otherwise stomping away the blues as such and having a good time not only as a result but also in the meanwhile. Which is also why whatever else hearing it makes you remember you also remember being somewhere among people wearing fine clothes and eating and laughing and talking and shucking and stuffing and jiving and conniving and making love. So sometimes it is also about the also and also of signifying and qualifying. Because sometimes, especially when you are still only a very young beginner standing at the edge of the dance floor getting yourself together to go over to where the girls (whose prerogative it is to say no) stand waiting to be approached and asked, it is also as if the orchestra were woofing at you. Back in the heyday of big dance halls like the Savoy, when the orchestra used to break into, say, Big John Special *(Fletcher Henderson, Decca DL 9228) or, say,* Cavernism *(Earl Hines, Decca DL 9221) or* Second Balcony Jump *(Earl Hines, Bandstand Records 7115) or* Wolverine Blues *(Louis Armstrong, Ace of Hearts AH 7) or* Miss Thing *(Count Basie, Columbia G 31224) or* Panassié Stomp *or* Shorty George, Every Tub *or* Dogging Around *(Count Basie, Decca DXSB 7170) or, say,* Cottontail *(Duke Ellington, RCA Victor LPM 1364),* Johnny Come Lately *(Duke Ellington, RCA Victor LPV 541),* Rockabye River, *erstwhile* Hop Skip Jump *(Duke Ellington, RCA Victor LPM 6009) it was as if you were being challenged (in a voice not unlike the rhapsodized thunder of a steam-snorting bluesteel express train highballing it*

257

hell for leather) to test your readiness, willingness, and nimbleness by escorting a girl of your choice around and up and down and across and crisscross the ballroom floor as if into and back again from the region of blue devils with all her finery intact, as if who else if not you were the storybook prince, as if whoever if not she were the fairytale princess.

Not that anybody has ever actually qualified once and for all. When the storybook hero is reported to have lived happily ever after his triumph over the dragon, it is not to be assumed that he is able to retire but rather that what he has been through should make him more insightful, more skillful, more resilient, and hence better prepared to cope with eventualities. Because there will always be other dragons, which after all are as much a part of the nature of things as is bad weather.

Nor has anybody ever been able to get rid of the blues forever either. You can only drive them away and keep them at bay for the time being. Because they are always there, as if always waiting and watching. So retirement is out of the question. But even so old pro that you have become, sometimes all you have to hear is the also and also of the drummer signifying on the high-hat cymbal, even in the distance (and it is as if it were the also and also of time itself whispering red alert as if in blue italics), and all you have to do to keep them in their proper place, which is deep in the dozens, is to pat your feet and snap your fingers.

Index

262

CREDITS

P. 11, Photo Files. P. 12, Photo Files (2). P. 12br, Wide World Photos, Inc. P. 13, Schomburg Collection, New York Public Library. Pp. 14, 15, Photo Files. P. 19, Photo Files. P. 19b, Harris Lewine Collection. P. 25, Bob Adelman. P. 26, Schomburg Collection, New York Public Library (2). Pp. 28, 29, Photo Files. P. 31, The Bettmann Archive. P. 32, Ernest Smith Collection (2). P. 33, Ernest Smith Collection (3). P. 33t, Photo Files. Pp. 34, 35, Harris Lewine Collection. P. 37, Frank Driggs Collection. P. 39, Charles Stewart. P. 40, Bob Parent. P. 41, The Bettmann Archive. P. 46, Photo Files. P. 47, Photo Files. P. 52, Photo Files. P. 53, Photo Files. P. 59, Harris Lewine Collection. P. 61, Ernest Smith Collection. P. 67, Photo Files. P. 71, Ernest Smith Collection. P. 72, Les Zeiger Collection. P. 73, Les Zeiger Collection. P. 80, Ernest Smith Collection. P. 84tl, Frank Driggs Collection. P. 84tr, Ernest Smith Collection. P. 84b, Photo Files. P. 85, Harris Lewine Collection. P. 88, Frank Driggs Collection. P. 89, Gjon Mili. P. 95tl, Photo Files. P. 95tr, Ernest Smith Collection. P. 97, Photo Files (2). P.100, Photo Files. P. 101, Culver Pictures, Inc. P. 103tl, Otto Hess Collection, New York Public Library. P. 103, Photo Files (2). P. 105t, Harris Lewine Collection. P. 105b, Gjon Mili. P. 107tl, Photo Files. P. 107tr, Ewing Galloway. P. 107b, Otto Hess Collection, New York Public Library. P. 109tl, Photo Files. P. 109tr, Charles Peterson. P. 109b, Photo Files (2). P. 110, Frank Driggs Collection. P. 111, Frank Driggs Collection (2). P. 112t, Ernest Smith Collection. P. 112b, Harris Lewine Collection. P. 113, Ramsey Archive/*Jazzmen*. P. 115, Frank Driggs Collection. P. 117tl, Photo Files. P. 117tr, Frank Driggs Collection. P. 117b, Photo Files. P. 119, Frederic Ramsey, Jr. (2). P. 120, Frederic Ramsey, Jr. (2). P. 121, The Bettmann Archive. Pp. 122, 123, Harris Lewine Collection. P. 134, Photo Files. P. 135, Photo Files. P. 141tl, Frank Driggs Collection. P. 141tr, Ernest Smith Collection. P. 141br, Photo Files. Pp. 142, 143, Ramsey Archive/*Jazzmen*. P. 145, Frank Driggs Collection. Pp. 146, 147, Photo Files. P. 153, Frank Driggs Collection (3). P. 154t, Frank Driggs Collection. P. 154b, Photo Files. P. 155, Ernest Smith Collection (2). Pp. 156, 157, Photo Files. P. 159t, Ernest Smith Collection. P. 159tr, Frank Driggs Collection. P. 159bl, Photo Files. P. 159br, Frank Driggs Collection. P. 160, 161, Otto Hess Collection, New York Public Library. P. 160, (inset) Photo Files. P. 162, Otto Hess Collection, New York Public Library. P. 163tl, Harris Lewine Collection. P. 163tr, Gjon Mili. P. 163b, Gjon Mili, Ernest Smith Collection. P. 165, Gjon Mili. P. 167tl, Photo Files. P. 167tr, Ernest Smith Collection. P. 167b, Frank Driggs Collection (2). P. 169, Otto Hess Collection, New York Public Library. P. 171, Photo Files (2). Pp. 172, 173, Photo Files. P. 175, Culver Pictures, Inc. P. 185, Frank Driggs Collection. P. 186, Photo Files. P. 187, Photo Files. P. 190, Don Perry, Hogan Jazz Archive, Tulane University. P. 191, Otto Hess Collection, New York Public Library. P. 192, Frank Driggs Collection. P. 193, Photo Files. Pp. 194, 195, Bernard M. Steinau, Hogan Jazz Archive, Tulane University. P. 197t, Wide World Photos, Inc. P. 197b, Courtesy of Esquire, Inc. Pp. 198, 199, Art Kane. P. 206, Photo Files. P. 207, Frank Driggs Collection. P. 210, Photo Files. P. 211, Carl Van Vechten, courtesy of Frank Driggs Collection. P. 213, Photo Files. P. 215t, Photo Files. P. 215b, Frank Driggs Collection. P. 216t, Ernest Smith Collection. P. 216m, Photo Files. P. 216b, Otto Hess Collection, New York Public Library. P. 217, Culver Pictures, Inc. Pp. 218, 219, Culver Pictures, Inc. P. 222t, Frank Driggs Collection (2). P. 222bl, Ernest Smith Collection. P. 222br, Photo Files. P. 223, Frank Driggs Collection. P. 228, Charles Stewart (3). P. 228br, Frank Driggs Collection. P. 229, Charles Stewart. P. 231, Bob Parent. P. 232t, Hugh Bell. P. 232b Otto Hess Collection, New York Public Library. P. 233, Frank Driggs Collection. P. 234, Harris Lewine Collection. P. 235, Harris Lewine Collection. P. 236, Photo Files. P. 237, Berk Costello. P. 239, Harris Lewine Collection. P. 240t, Gjon Mili. P. 240bl, Gjon Mili. P. 240br, Otto Hess Collection, New York Public Library. P. 241 Photo Files (2). P. 242tl, Otto Hess Collection, New York Public Library. P. 242tr, Herman Leonard/Charles Stewart Collection. P. 242br, Harris Lewine Collection. P. 243, Photo Files (2). Pp. 246, 247, Photo Files. Pp. 248, 249, Hogan Jazz Archive, Tulane University. P.253, Otto Hess Collection, New York Public Library. Record labels reproduced from the Les Zeiger Collection.